LANGUAGE-BASED
LEARNING DISABILITIES

Patricia W. Newhall

LANDMARK SCHOOL OUTREACH PROGRAM

PROFESSIONAL DEVELOPMENT FOR EDUCATORS

The information and educational interventions presented in this book are for classroom use and should not be construed as substitutions or replacements for evaluations and recommendations from physicians, pyschologists, or neuropsychologists.

Individuals pictured in this book bear no relation to examples or profiles in this book.

To reference this publication, please use the following citation:

Newhall, P. W. (2012). Language-based learning disabilities. In P. W. Newhall (Ed.), *Language-based teaching series*. Prides Crossing, MA: Landmark School Outreach Program.

Contents

Materials for Reproduction

The resources listed below may be photocopied from this book for personal or classroom use. They are also available online for printing or customizing at www.landmarkoutreach.org/lbld-resources. When you open this page, enter the username **(lbld)** and the password **(OUTREACH)**.

Online Resource Available

About Us
Landmark School Outreach Program

Established in 1977 as the professional development arm of Landmark School, Landmark Outreach's mission is to empower students through their teachers. Landmark Outreach serves both general and special education professionals, with the goal of sharing knowledge and strategies that contribute to students' classroom success. Landmark Outreach provides language-based consulting and program design in collaboration with schools and districts, summer Professional Development Institutes, and publications. Information about Outreach programs and publications is available at landmarkoutreach.org.

Founded in 1971, Landmark School is recognized internationally as a leader in the field of language-based learning disabilities. A coeducational boarding and day school for elementary, middle, and high school students, Landmark individualizes instruction for each student and emphasizes the development of language and learning skills within a highly structured living and learning environment. Information about Landmark School is available online at landmarkschool.org.

Introduction
Language-Based Teaching Series

As educators, we are deeply invested in helping young people reach their potential. The curricula we design and the instruction we deliver are informed by our goal of fostering students' development into individuals who are intellectually engaged in the world of ideas, active in their communities, morally and spiritually aware, and physically healthy. We coach our students to become independent thinkers and creative problem-solvers and decision-makers who communicate effectively and act with responsible purpose. Often, though, our lofty goals are obscured by the daily grind of lesson planning, grading, advising, coaching, and the myriad other responsibilities teachers commonly shoulder.

This series is about helping students reach their academic potential. Young people arrive in our classrooms with biological makeups and life experiences that influence both what and how they learn. Some students have learning disabilities; some do not. All students have potential, and all students need our help to reach it.

As it takes a village to raise a child, it takes a school to train a scholar. We all – faculty, staff, and administrators – are responsible for facilitating each student's educational rearing. Sometimes, in our urgency to ready students for the competitive adult world, we forget that we are teaching young people who need models, explicit instruction, and guided practice in order to gain independence. As one school's principal commented, "Too frequently, we lose sight of the student for the assignment."

Some students come to us with a full complement of academic skills and enthusiasm for schoolwork. We praise the quality of their independent work, and in our own minds hold them up as the standard by which we judge other students. Many students fall short, and we wonder why. Our wondering leads us to all sorts of assumptions.

The Language-Based Teaching Series offers information and practical resources to help teachers and administrators understand and support the students who fall short of expectations. From a synthesis of research on learning to insights gained in the classroom, the series aims to support educators' efforts to help all students learn effectively. Each book focuses on one topic, organizes chapters around *what to know* and *what to do,* and provides printed checklists, questionnaires, and other tools that can be reproduced as-is or accessed online and customized. These materials are intended to spark ideas and help with understanding students' thinking, scaffolding learning, and implementing skills-based instruction.

Of course, there are no quick fixes for students with learning difficulties, and no single book or program can address all learners' needs. This series aims to get teachers thinking broadly about students' strengths and weaknesses, how they learn, and what helps them gain essential skills. To learn when new books in the series are released, visit landmarkoutreach.org and join the Outreach mailing list.

Landmark's
Six Teaching Principles™

At the heart of Landmark's instructional strategies and programs are six teaching principles.

PROVIDE OPPORTUNITIES FOR SUCCESS

Providing students with opportunities for success is key. Failure and poor self-esteem often result when teachers challenge students beyond their ability. Landmark begins teaching students at their current level of ability. This approach improves basic skills and enhances confidence. As Landmark teachers introduce each new skill, they provide basic examples and assignments to build confidence and keep students from becoming overwhelmed. As the information becomes more challenging, teachers assign students easier problems to supplement the more difficult ones. In this way, those students who are having trouble with the material complete at least part of the assignment while they work at understanding and learning to apply new information. Teachers give themselves permission to provide students with whatever structure is necessary to help students be successful, such as study guides for tests, templates for writing, and guidelines for projects. Only with a solid foundation of basic skills and confidence can students make progress.

USE MULTISENSORY APPROACHES

Multisensory teaching is effective for all students. In general, it means presenting all information to students via three sensory modalities: visual, auditory, and tactile. Visual presentation techniques include graphic organizers for structuring writing and pictures for reinforcing instruction; auditory presentation techniques include conducting thorough discussions and reading aloud; tactile presentation techniques include manipulating blocks and creating paragraphs about objects students can hold in their hands. Overall, implementing a multisensory approach to teaching is not difficult; in fact, many teachers use such an approach. It is important, however, to be aware of the three sensory modes and to plan to integrate them every day.

MICRO-UNIT AND STRUCTURE TASKS

Effective teaching involves breaking information down into its smallest units and providing clear guidelines for all assignments. This is especially important for students with learning disabilities. "Micro-uniting" and structuring are elements of directive teaching, which Landmark consistently uses with students. Micro-uniting means analyzing the parts of a task or assignment and teaching those parts one step at a time. Teachers organize information so students can see and follow the steps clearly and sequentially. As students learn to micro-unit for themselves, they become less likely to give up on tasks that appear confusing or overwhelming. Consequently, these strategies enable students to proceed in a step-by-step, success-oriented way.

ENSURE AUTOMATIZATION THROUGH PRACTICE AND REVIEW

Automatization is the process of learning and assimilating a task or skill so completely that it can be consistently completed with little or no conscious attention. Repetition and review (spiraling) are critical. Sometimes, students appear to understand a concept, only to forget it a day, week, or month later. It is not until students have automatized a skill that they can effectively remember and use it as a foundation for new tasks. Teachers must therefore provide ample opportunities for students to repeat and review learned material. For example, the Landmark writing process emphasizes practice and consistency. Students always brainstorm, map/outline, draft, and proofread in the same way. This provides them with an ongoing, consistent review of learned skills.

PROVIDE MODELS

Providing models is simple, yet very important. It is one of the most effective teaching techniques. Models are concrete examples of what teachers expect. This does not mean that teachers are doing assignments for students. Models are standards to which students can compare their own work. A model or example of a completed assignment serves as a springboard for students to begin the assignment. For example, teachers should give students a model of a sequential paragraph when teaching basic sequential paragraph writing.

INCLUDE STUDENTS IN THE LEARNING PROCESS

Students are not passive receptacles to fill with information. They come to class with their own frames of reference. Their unique experiences and knowledge affect them as learners and should be taken into account. Therefore, during every exercise, teachers should accept student input as much as possible. They should justify assignments, accept suggestions, solicit ideas, and provide ample time for students to share ideas. Teachers should include students in assessing their own progress by reviewing test results, written reports, and educational plans. Creating and improvising opportunities to involve students in the learning process allows students to become aware of how they learn and why certain skills benefit them. As a result, students are motivated and more likely to apply those skills when working independently. In short, an included student becomes an invested student who is eager to learn.

I never teach my pupils, I only attempt to provide the conditions
in which they can learn.
- Albert Einstein, educator and theoretical physicist

Chapter I
Language-Based Learning Disability

WHAT TO KNOW

The development of fluent language skills is rooted in complex cognitive processes that include attention, auditory and visual perception and processing, memory, and executive function. Students who have difficulty in any of these areas may also have difficulty acquiring the facility with language that school requires. To understand a reading selection, for example, students must be able to pay attention to the task of reading, decode the words, retrieve vocabulary and related knowledge from memory, and recognize the syntax and structure of discourse.

The Basics

Language-based learning disability (LBLD) refers to a spectrum of difficulties related to the understanding and use of spoken and written language. LBLD is a common cause of students' academic struggles because weak language skills impede comprehension and communication, which are the basis for most school activity.

Like all learning disabilities, LBLD results from a combination of neurobiological differences (variations in the way an individual's brain functions) and environmental factors (e.g., the learning setting , the type of instruction). The key to supporting students with LBLD is knowing how to adjust curriculum and instruction to ensure they develop proficient language and literacy skills. Most individuals with LBLD need instruction that is specialized, explicit, structured, and

When teachers know how to celebrate students' strong skills and remediate their weak ones using skills-based curriculum and instruction, students' lives can change.

multisensory, as well as ongoing, guided practice aimed at remediating their specific areas of weakness.

LBLD can manifest as a wide variety of language difficulties with different levels of severity. One student may have difficulty sounding out words for reading or spelling, but no difficulty with oral expression or listening comprehension. Another may struggle with all three. The spectrum of LBLD ranges from students who experience minor interferences that may be addressed in class to students who need specialized, individualized attention throughout the school day in order to develop fluent language skills.

Academic Proficiency

Academic proficiency develops in relation to students' increasing skills and abilities. Its three interrelated elements, shown in Figure 1, are coordinated by the individual's executive function. Executive function enables students to maintain focus, progress, and motivation; make connections with existing knowledge; recognize when comprehension falters; and apply strategies to modulate frustration and resolve lapses in understanding.

Language and literacy skills include listening, speaking, reading and writing. Study skills include flexible and appropriate use of strategies for managing materials, time, and language. Self-efficacy (the belief that one's actions are related to outcomes) includes skills in self-awareness, self-assessment, and self-advocacy. All of these skills are coordinated by executive function, which is the brain's super-manager and empowers students to set goals, marshall the various internal and external resources needed to meet them, and make adjustments to ensure accomplishment.

Most students with LBLD develop academic proficiency only when they are taught skills within a supportive environment of curriculum and instruction designed to meet their specific needs. When teachers know how to celebrate students' strong skills and remediate thei weak ones using skills-based curriculum and instruction, students' lives can change. The first step to

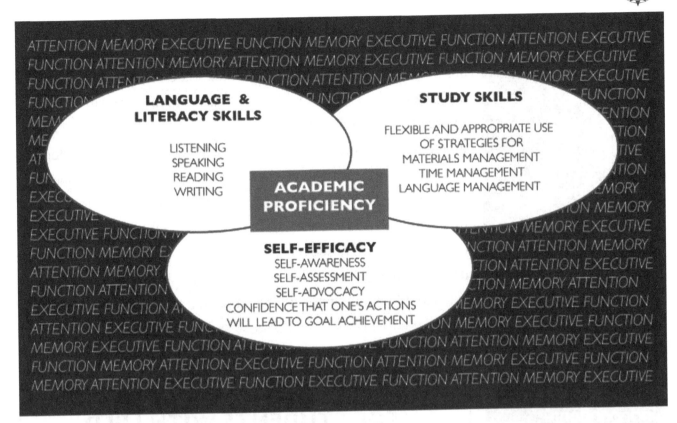

Figure 1. Elements of Academic Proficiency

empowering students with LBLD is to understand how and when LBLD impacts their school experience and why language-based teaching works.

Emergence and Signs of Language-Based Difficulties

Children naturally develop skills at their own pace, and most students have difficulty learning from time to time. To assess whether a student's performance in a skill area warrants concern, we must take into account typical development patterns. We expect preschool children to have difficulty tying their shoes, cutting out pictures from magazines, adding numbers, and writing neatly. Middle school students should be able to do these things quite easily. It is persistent difficulty in one or more skill areas that requires investigation. Even so, the level of struggle that calls for investigation does not emerge at a predictable time in child development; rather, difficulties may appear at any time from preschool

> Many students progress through elementary school with few issues. As they transition into middle school, high school, or even college, the demands for using language rise, as do expectations for independent learning.

through adulthood.

While some students with languge-based learning disabilities are diagnosed very young, many other students progress through early elementary school with few issues. As they transition into middle school, high school, or even college, the demands for language rise, as do expectations for independent learning. Students who performed competently in structured, skills-based, supportive classrooms may find themselves floundering as they try to manage their school and homework with less individual guidance from teachers. They may suddenly seem anxious, frustrated, angry, or defeated about school. This level of change warrants investigation, and should not automatically be attributed to typical adolescent behavior.

COMMON DIFFICULTIES FOR STUDENTS WITH LBLD

LISTENING	SOCIAL SKILLS
SPEAKING	ATTENTION
READING	MEMORY
WRITING	ORGANIZATION
SPELLING	PERSEVERANCE
MATHEMATICS	SELF-REGULATION

Sometimes difficulties emerge because the compensatory strategies students used in the past stop working. Many bright students with learning disabilities go to great lengths to mask their struggles. Their intelligence enables them to compensate for lack of skill in one area with talents in other areas. A student might be a terrific talker and demonstrate solid knowledge in class discussions. Why would the teacher guess this student cannot read fluently? While students' capacity to adapt is admirable, the cost is high. Too often, they enter middle and high school with elementary-level reading and writing skills. The fact is, if schools took the time to administer literacy screening assessments to all students at least once each year, those at risk could be identified, provided with remedial instruction, and offered accommodations to help them succeed in class.

Many screening assessments are commercially available, and easy to administer and score. Curriculum-based measurement (CBM) can also be used to screen students. Excellent free resources for CBM are available online at www.interventioncentral.org. In addition to screenings, students offer a rich source of information about their learning strengths and struggles - if we take the time to ask. The learning questionnaires at the end of this chapter show one example of how to ask students to self-report.

> If schools took the time to administer literacy screening assessments to all students at least once each year, those at risk could be identified, provided with remedial instruction, and offered accommodations to help them succeed in class.

LANGUAGE DIFFICULTY OR DISABILITY?

Language difficulties are not always language disabilities. In order for a student to be eligible for special education services guided by an individualized education plan (IEP), he or she must be diagnosed with a disability. Under the Individuals with Disabilities Education Act (IDEA), a language-based learning disability is considered a specific learning disability (SLD). A diagnosis of SLD means the student's difficulties are *not* the result of:

- ENVIRONMENTAL, CULTURAL, OR ECONOMIC DISADVANTAGE

- DIFFICULTY ACQUIRING ENGLISH AS A SECOND LANGUAGE

- A MOTOR DISABILITY

- A VISUAL OR HEARING ACUITY PROBLEM

- IMPAIRED COGNITIVE FUNCTION (THOUGH SEVERE FORMS OF LBLD CAN AFFECT PERFORMANCE ON ASSESSMENTS OF COGNITIVE FUNCTION)

STUDENT PROFILES

STUDENT PROFILES

The student profiles section of each chapter introduces different facets of five students: Lan, Carlos, Ayanna, Elijah, and Jason. Each experiences difficulties in school that teachers must analyze and address. The profiles are composites of several actual students whose names have been changed here.

Students have unique learning profiles that reflect their educational experience, their learning, thinking, and personality styles, and their particular areas of need for language acquisition and use. All students who struggle in school - particularly those with LBLD - benefit from structured, multisensory, skills-based instruction. Each requires individualized instruction targeted at his or her specific needs. The student profiles in this book are included to encourage teachers' thinking about students in their own classes.

Consider Background and Current Performance

As you read about each student's background and current performance, keep in mind the following questions:

WHY MIGHT THIS STUDENT BE STRUGGLING?

WHAT IS PREVENTING THIS STUDENT FROM LEARNING EFFECTIVELY?

WHAT STEPS WOULD I TAKE TO SUPPORT THIS STUDENT?

Also think about your own students:

WHO AMONG MY STUDENTS IS NOT MEETING EXPECTATIONS?

WHAT STEPS HAVE I TAKEN TO SUPPORT THESE STUDENTS?

WHAT SHOULD MY NEXT STEPS BE?

Lan, Grade 2

LAN is the only child in a two-parent, English-speaking household in a small city. Her teacher is concerned about her reading, writing, math, and social skills. Lan's reading skills fall significantly below grade level in spite of her work in a small, supportive reading group over the past two years. In writing, she demonstrates good penmanship and produces lengthy compositions; however, her spelling, vocabulary, syntax, and organization of ideas make her writing very difficult to understand. In math, she has good number sense but struggles with word and logic problems. Lan focuses intently on all her schoolwork and becomes angry when she makes mistakes or when teachers offer support or suggestions for improvement. Lan's homework is always complete, and her hands-on projects demonstrate understanding of the concepts taught in class. Socially, Lan struggles. Though she seeks out others for play and projects, she is often removed due to verbal and physical altercations.

Carlos, Grade 4

CARLOS is one of five children in a two-parent, bilingual household in a rural community. He was diagnosed with attention deficit hyperactivity disorder (ADHD) in kindergarten and takes medication for this condition. Carlos's academic performance in early elementary school was strong, but he is having difficulty with the demands of the fourth-grade curriculum. His reading assessments show solid decoding skills, but his written work is often incomplete and he has not mastered his math facts in spite of having good mathematical thinking skills. Carlos's teachers feel that he is not putting enough effort into his work. Carlos has many friends, is a talented athlete in several youth sports, and is known as "LEGO® man" because he spends his free time building robots and inventing machines using LEGO and electronic parts.

Ayanna, Grade 6

AYANNA is one of two children in a single-parent, English-speaking family that recently relocated to a small town. Her mother reports that Ayanna was late in learning to talk in sentences and in learning to read. In second grade, she was diagnosed with a reading disorder and received small group tutoring for two years to help her catch up. She decodes at grade level now and is not on an individualized education plan at her new school. Her teachers report that Ayanna is an attentive and highly organized student who puts tremendous effort into her work. However, she achieves little success except on memorization tasks. She recently won the

STUDENT PROFILES

schoolwide spelling bee. Though she decodes accurately and seems to listen in class, her notes and oral answers do not demonstrate good comprehension. Ayanna's writing shows poor vocabulary, weak syntax, and difficulty staying on topic or elaborating on ideas, and her reading quiz scores are low. Ayanna also experiences social difficulty; her teachers note that she tries to fit in but is often ignored and sometimes teased by her peers.

ELIJAH is one of two foster children in a two-parent, English-speaking family in a midsized city. He has a history of being abused and in trouble with the law. Child services took custody of him when he was found living alone in a shack beside the rail tracks. His current living situation is his first foster placement, and it has been working out positively for close to two years. The quality of Elijah's schoolwork varies from failing grades to perfect scores. He takes notes in class and participates in discussions, but completing homework is a major challenge. He sometimes falls asleep in class. He has difficulty deciding on writing topics and in organizing and elaborating on his ideas. His in-class test scores are generally very low, but longer term projects are stronger if he remembers to do them. He has tremendous math anxiety and works at a very slow pace. Elijah's oral language is marked by its slow pace, pauses, and frequent difficulty with word finding. He is a talented actor and musician.

Elijah, Grade 8

JASON is one of four children in a single-parent, Spanish-speaking household in a large city. He is fluent in English. His teachers note that he seems to have a good understanding of concepts in the content areas based on the work he does in class, especially in math and chemistry. Though never a top student, Jason's grades have been declining since he started high school. He is failing his classes because his test and essay scores are very low and he is not doing homework consistently. Jason has a solid social group, and occasionally participates in school activities when his work schedule allows it. Recently, he has expressed a desire to leave high school and pursue full-time work in the landscaping business he started with his older brother.

Jason, Grade 10

I want students to engage the way a clutch on a car gets engaged: an engine can be running, making appropriate noises, burning fuel and creating exhaust fumes, but unless the clutch is engaged, nothing moves. It's all sound and smoke, and nobody gets anywhere.

\- Robert L. Fried, educator and author

In Their Own Words
Students with LBLD Talk about School

I'm not good at school. I'm good at baseball.

Elias, age 8

There are a lot of ways to be smart; I guess school's just not mine. I wish it was but I'd rather be on stage anyway. I have no problems there, and it's fun and I learn a lot.

Pedro, age 12

I'm pretty sure I work harder than anybody else. Some of my friends don't even study for tests and they get As and Bs. Sometimes I get a good grade.

Monica, age 13

I've been going to school triple-time for most of my life because I have learning disabilities. I go to regular school, then I go to tutoring around four or five times a week and in the summer too. It's rather tiresome.

Lily, age 16

WHAT TO DO

No matter their grade level, the range of students' skills and knowledge is dramatic. In order to nurture their educational lives, we need to know them well: where they come from and what their lives are like, what they like and dislike about school, and what they are good at and what they find difficult. We also need to learn about students' language and literacy skills. Quite a few students enter our classrooms with individualized education plans (IEPs) in place, which provide clear guidance on the skills they need to develop and the accommodations and modifications we are required to provide. Most arrive without this guidance. What strategies can we use to gather useful information in a timely way?

Learning Questionnaires

Questionnaires are easy to design and can provide a wealth of information. Free online survey programs can be wonderfully helpful, but plain old pencil and paper work just as well. Many teachers use questionnaires at the beginning of each year or term to get specific information that will help guide their instruction.

Online Resource Available

The questionnaires that follow provide teachers with immediate feedback on students' perceptions of their academic strengths and needs in five areas: listening, speaking, reading, writing, and mathematics. Students' perceptions alone are a rich source of diagnostic information. When compared with actual performance in class, students' perceptions add insight into their self-awareness and self-efficacy.

The questionnaires provide a good entry point for implementing formative assessment practices. They also provide a useful starting point for conferences with students or parents. They should not replace the formal diagnostic assessment tools to be used with students suspected of having learning disabilities. Modify or print these learning questionnaires at www.landmarkoutreach.org/lbld-resources. When you open this page, enter the username (**lbld**) and the password (**OUTREACH**).

LEARNING QUESTIONNAIRE

Learning Questionnaire: Elementary

Name:

Date:

Directions

Put a check mark beside each sentence that describes you.

READING

	I like to read to myself.
	I like to look at the pictures in books more than reading.
	I like to read out loud.
	I like it when someone reads to me.
	I think I'm a good reader.

WRITING

	I write a lot when I have an assignment.
	Most of the time I can spell the words I need and follow sentence rules.
	I have a lot of ideas for writing, but it's hard to put them into words.
	Writing is really hard for me.
	I think I'm a good writer.

TURN TO THE NEXT PAGE>

LISTENING

	I understand what the teacher says.
	I understand what kids say in class and at recess.
	Sometimes I miss what people say and have to ask them to repeat it.
	It is hard for me to pay attention when others are talking.
	I think I'm a good listener.

SPEAKING

	I like to ask and answer questions in class.
	I like to explain things to other people.
	I have a hard time remembering words when I'm talking.
	Sometimes people don't understand what I'm trying to say.
	I think I'm good at talking about my ideas.

MATH

	I figure out math problems pretty easily.
	I have a hard time remembering what to do when I have to solve different problems.
	I get frustrated when I have to do math.
	It is hard for me to spend a lot of time figuring out math problems.
	I think I'm good at math.

LEARNING QUESTIONNAIRE

THIS IS THE END OF THE QUESTIONNAIRE.

Learning Questionnaire: Middle and High School

Name:

Date:

Directions

1. In each section, circle the number next to the statement that best describes you.

2. Complete the Interpret Your Learning Questionnaire and read about what to do next.

READING

Reading for School

0	I read quickly and understand and remember what I've read.
1	Most of the time I understand and remember what I've read.
2	It takes me a long time to read, and when I do, I often forget what I've read or don't totally understand it.
3	I often avoid reading for school because it's too much or too difficult.

Reading for Pleasure

0	I like to read and do a lot beyond what is required.
1	I read fairly regularly – a few magazines, blogs, and an occasional book.
2	Most of the reading I do is e-mails, textbooks, and Facebook.
3	I don't particularly enjoy reading.

WRITING

Writing for School

0	Writing comes fairly easily to me, and I do very well on my written assignments.
1	I'm a decent writer, and I work really hard at it. I get passing grades on my written assignments.
2	It takes me a long time to get my thoughts organized and written, and I sometimes don't do well on written assignments.
3	I dislike writing for school because it takes too long and I generally don't do well on my written assignments.

Writing for Pleasure

0	I really enjoy writing, and I write a lot when I have time after schoolwork.
1	I write fairly regularly, sometimes for fun or for a school activity, such as a newspaper or literary magazine.
2	Most of the writing I do is very short – texting or posting on line.
3	I don't particularly enjoy writing and I do as little of it as I can.

CONTINUED ON THE NEXT PAGE>

LEARNING QUESTIONNAIRE

LISTENING and SPEAKING	
Listening and Speaking in Class	
0	I remember what I've heard in lectures and I participate in class discussions. Both help me understand new ideas and information.
1	I like to listen to lectures and I sometimes participate in class discussions. In order to learn from these, I have to take notes or I won't remember the information.
2	I don't mind listening, and I sometimes answer questions. Sometimes I lose track of the conversation or find my attention wandering.
3	I don't like listening to lectures or class discussions or participating in class. It doesn't really help me learn.
Listening and Speaking Outside of Class	
0	I really enjoy conversations. I'm a good listener, and I like it when others listen to what I have to say. I enjoy spending a lot of free time talking with my friends or family.
1	I like conversations, and I prefer to do most of the listening. People say I'm quiet.
2	I like conversations when I can contribute a lot. I try to be a good listener. People say I talk a lot.
3	I don't much enjoy conversations. Sometimes it's hard to follow what people are saying, or to think of the right things to say before it's too late. It's easier to be by myself, or to be in a group where I don't have to say anything.

MATHEMATICS	
Mathematics in School	
0	I am good at math. I do well in class and on tests, and I enjoy taking on new math challenges.
1	I like math and most of the time I do well at it in school.
2	Math isn't really my thing, but if I put in the time and effort I do OK in it.
3	I don't like math much at all, and I don't get good grades in it.
Mathematics Outside of School	
0	I really enjoy numbers and math. I have no problems making change, managing my money, or calculating sale prices or tax. I think mathematically, whether it's seeing geometrical shapes in my surroundings or translating information into equations or graphs.
1	I like numbers and math. I find the basic math I need to do outside of school pretty easy. When people ask me to apply math to some activity or project, I can do it if I think about it.
2	I'm OK with math. I can do the basics, but it's hard for me to think of things mathematically.
3	I don't like math and I'm not very good at it. It takes me a while to do mental math, like making change or calculating sales.

LEARNING QUESTIONNAIRE

CONTINUED ON THE NEXT PAGE>

LEARNING QUESTIONNAIRE

Interpret Your Learning Questionnaire

Totals: Add up your score for each section, and enter it below.

1. Reading Section Total _____

2. Writing Section Total _____

3. Listening & Speaking Section Total _____

4. Mathematics Section Total _____

What to Do Next

If you scored 0 or 1 in any section
Talk to your teacher about taking on additional challenges!

If you scored 2 or 3 in any section
You're probably doing just fine in that subject area.

If your scored 4, 5 or 6 in any section
Talk to your teachers, counselor, and parents/caregivers. You may need to be taught in a different way to be successful.

Comments:

Chapter 2
The Language of Language

WHAT TO KNOW

Most learning in school takes place through the medium of language, and most students who struggle in school have difficulty in some area of language. The struggle may be in the area of perception, of processing and comprehension, or of organization and production. It may be in all three. A basic understanding of the language of language can help orient us to LBLD and where students may experience problems.

Language skills can be categorized into four interrelated areas: listening, speaking, reading, and writing. Listening and reading comprehension are *receptive language skills*. Speaking and writing are *expressive language skills*. Figure 2 shows the relationships.

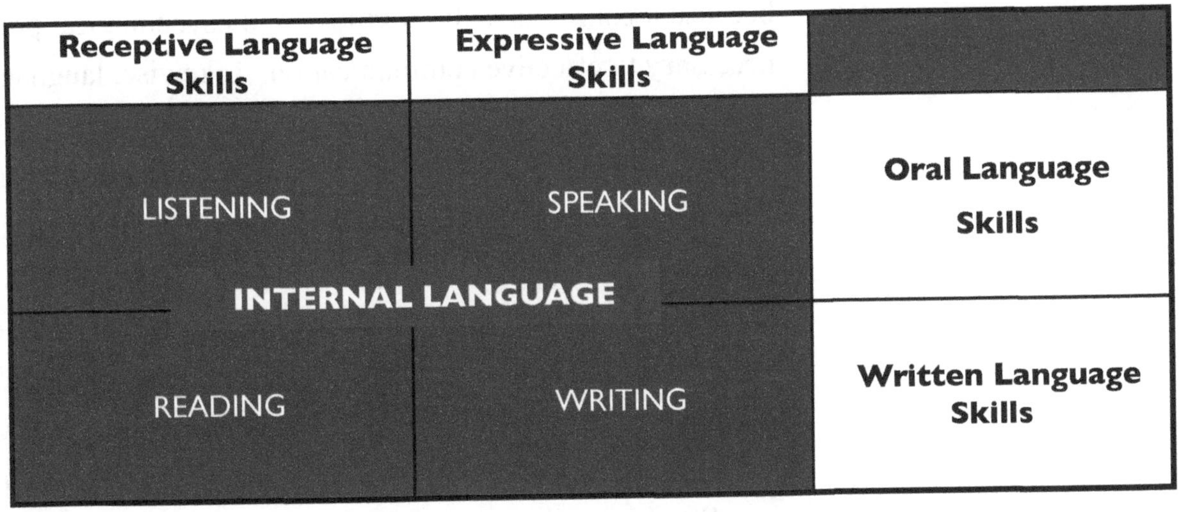

Receptive Language Skills	Expressive Language Skills	
LISTENING	SPEAKING	**Oral Language Skills**
INTERNAL LANGUAGE		
READING	WRITING	**Written Language Skills**

Figure 2. The language box.

> To a great extent, proficiency in the areas of language (listening, speaking, reading, and writing) depends upon executive function and mastery of the five linguistic areas (morphemes, phonemes, syntax, lexicon, and semantics) within a framework of understanding and producing oral and written discourse.

The areas of language develop in an overlapping way, and interferences in the development of one area can cause difficulty in others. For instance, students who do not read fluently or frequently do not develop as robust a vocabulary or fund of knowledge as their peers. If their difficulty is in the area of processing language (e.g., dyslexia) and they do not receive appropriate remedial instruction, they never catch up with their fluently reading peers (Shaywitz, 2003, p. 34). They may have increasing difficulty with comprehension, and their writing may fall below age-appropriate expectations. The gaps widen over time. This phenomenon, known as the *Matthew effect* (Merton, 1968; Stanovich, 1986), highlights the importance of identifying the causes of school difficulty early on and not assuming that a student will outgrow the difficulty. Early identification and appropriate intervention can prevent these widening achievement gaps.

Facets of Language

Language becomes coherent communication through a dynamic interaction of its facets. From the smallest speech sounds, called phonemes, to complex communication, called discourse, our brains are constantly perceiving, processing, managing, and producing language in order to learn and communicate with others. Figure 3 summarizes important linguistic terminology.

Executive function is key in the mastery of language skill because it coordinates the cognitive and psychological processes necessary to effective communication. Likewise, language skill supports executive skill development because executive function is mediated by our capacity to use productive internal language.

To a great extent, proficiency in the areas of language (listening, speaking, reading, and writing) depends upon executive function and mastery of the five linguistic areas (morphemes, phonemes, syntax, lexicon, and semantics) within a framework of understanding and producing oral and written discourse. Additionally, effective oral discourse requires appropriate prosody and pragmatics. Effective written language, requires appropriate use of the conventions of written language including word spacing, capitalization, punctuation, and spelling. For instance, students who struggle to process phonemes may misperceive and misunderstand oral language, mispronounce words, and struggle with reading and spelling. In fact, most reading disorders result from differences in the way the individual's brain processes phonemes, which helps explain the origins of the term *phonological processing disorder.* Without appropriate individualized instruction for the phonemic difficulty, language proficiency is impeded.

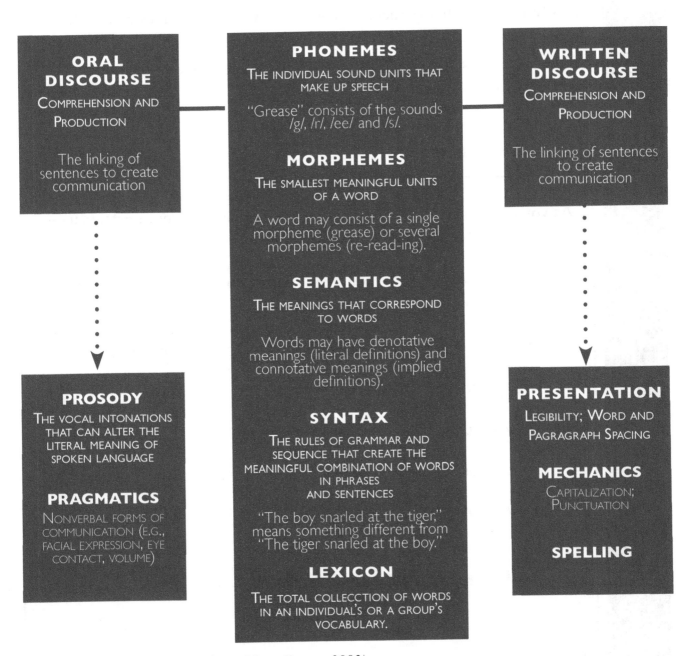

ORAL DISCOURSE

COMPREHENSION AND PRODUCTION

The linking of sentences to create communication

PHONEMES

THE INDIVIDUAL SOUND UNITS THAT MAKE UP SPEECH

"Grease" consists of the sounds /g/, /r/, /ee/ and /s/.

MORPHEMES

THE SMALLEST MEANINGFUL UNITS OF A WORD

A word may consist of a single morpheme (grease) or several morphemes (re-read-ing).

SEMANTICS

THE MEANINGS THAT CORRESPOND TO WORDS

Words may have denotative meanings (literal definitions) and connotative meanings (implied definitions).

SYNTAX

THE RULES OF GRAMMAR AND SEQUENCE THAT CREATE THE MEANINGFUL COMBINATION OF WORDS IN PHRASES AND SENTENCES

"The boy snarled at the tiger," means something different from "The tiger snarled at the boy."

LEXICON

THE TOTAL COLLECCTION OF WORDS IN AN INDIVIDUAL'S OR A GROUP'S VOCABULARY.

WRITTEN DISCOURSE

COMPREHENSION AND PRODUCTION

The linking of sentences to create communication

PROSODY

THE VOCAL INTONATIONS THAT CAN ALTER THE LITERAL MEANING OF SPOKEN LANGUAGE

PRAGMATICS

NONVERBAL FORMS OF COMMUNICATION (E.G., FACIAL EXPRESSION, EYE CONTACT, VOLUME)

PRESENTATION

LEGIBILITY; WORD AND PAGRAGRAPH SPACING

MECHANICS

CAPITALIZATION; PUNCTUATION

SPELLING

Figure 3. Linguistic terms (Adapted from Stacey, 2003).

STUDENT PROFILES

STUDENT PROFILES

The student profiles section of each chapter introduces different facets of five students: Lan, Carlos, Ayanna, Elijah, and Jason. Each experiences difficulties in school that teachers must analyze and address. The profiles are composites of several actual students whose names have been changed here.

Students have unique learning profiles that reflect their educational experience, their learning, thinking, and personality styles, and their particular areas of need for language acquisition and use. All students who struggle in school - particularly those with LBLD - benefit from structured, multisensory, skills-based instruction. Each requires individualized instruction targeted at his or her specific needs. The student profiles in this book are included to encourage teachers' thinking about students in their own classes.

Diagnostic Assessment

As you read about each student's background and current performance, keep in mind the following questions:

IN WHAT WAYS DOES THE DIAGNOSTIC ASSESSMENT CONFIRM OR CONTRADICT WHAT I KNOW ABOUT THIS STUDENT?

ARE THERE OTHER ASSESSMENTS THAT PROVIDE HELPFUL INFORMATION?

WHAT NEXT STEPS WOULD I TAKE TO EMPOWER THIS STUDENT?

Also think about your own students:

WHO AMONG MY STUDENTS IS NOT MEETING EXPECTATIONS?

WHAT KINDS OF INFORMAL ASSESSMENT COULD I DO IN ORDER TO FIGURE OUT WHAT IS CAUSING DIFFICULTY?

WHAT STEPS CAN I TAKE TO EMPOWER MY STRUGGLING STUDENTS?

**Lan,
Grade 2**

LAN has received reading intervention with increasing intensity since kindergarten but made minimal progress. She was referred for diagnostic assessment as well as a behavior evaluation. Lan's cognitive ability scores range from above average to superior, and show a wide gap between her verbal (average) and nonverbal (superior) abilities. Her performance on academic assessments does not reflect her cognitive abilities. With the exception of reading, her scores fall in the average range. A behavior evaluation concluded that the trigger for Lan's difficulties is frustration with making herself understood to her peers and adults. A speech-language evaluation then indicated that Lan has a severe phonological processing deficit and an expressive language disorder.

**Carlos,
Grade 4**

Several months of various interventions to help CARLOS improve his work quality and homework completion resulted in only marginal improvement, and Carlos resisted the additional help. An educational evaluation found that his verbal and nonverbal cognitive abilities fall in the average range overall. Of note is his superior performance on tasks of visual perception and his extremely low performance on tasks requiring attention, working memory, and processing speed. Academic skills testing indicated performance at or above grade level in all areas. The evaluation included this comment from Carlos: "If I could do all my work in a quiet place and someone told me exactly what to do, I'd be a better student." Carlos's parents and teachers completed ADHD questionnaires as part of this evaluation. Results indicate that Carlos's ADHD is not being adequately addressed, and that he is struggling as a result of weak executive function. A plan to re-evaluate his medication and make changes in instruction was recommended.

**Ayanna,
Grade 6**

AYANNA decodes above grade level, but reads out loud with little inflection in her voice. She has difficulty answering comprehension questions, whether she reads a passage herself or it is read to her. Her teacher invited Ms. L., a speech-language pathologist, to observe class and examine Ayanna's written work. Ms. L. expressed concerns about Ayanna's language and social development and recommended a full evaluation. Assessments showed Ayanna's cognitive abilities to be below average on verbal tasks, average on nonverbal tasks,

STUDENT PROFILES

and significantly below grade level in all areas of academic performance. Further testing indicated that though Ayanna's dyslexia was remediated in terms of decoding speed and accuracy, her receptive language weaknesses interfere with her comprehension of both written and oral language. The difficulties with oral expressive language and writing skills highlight Ayanna's difficulties acquiring and using vocabulary, manipulating syntax, and generating clear discourse. She was diagnosed with a receptive-expressive language disorder.

ELIJAH'S diagnostic assessment showed that his cognitive abilities fall in the high average range, but his weak working memory and slow processing speed interfere with successful performance. Elijah has also been diagnosed with ADHD and exhibits many behaviors consistent with weak executive function, particularly in sustaining effort and focus. Additionally, a speech-language evaluation concluded that Elijah has an expressive language disorder. The combined challenges of Elijah's ADHD and expressive language disorder make it difficult for him to achieve the level of academic independence expected of an eighth-grade student, especially in terms of homework and longer reading and writing assignments.

Elijah, Grade 8

In a recent after-school meeting, JASON'S English teacher asked him to read aloud from the novel the class was studying. Her intent was to show him how to use a quote from the reading to support an assertion about the main character. Jason was unable to read the passage fluently. He explained that reading had always been difficult for him, but that he was able to get by until high school. Jason's teacher arranged for the special education director to administer a reading assessment. It showed Jason's decoding skill to be at about the fourth-grade level. Additional assessments determined that Jason's listening comprehension is quite good, but his ability to express himself in speaking and writing is also limited. The school determined that Jason should receive additional instruction for a time before referring him for a full evaluation. The interventions were not enough to bring Jason's skills to a proficient level. When an educational evaluation was completed several months later, Jason was diagnosed with a reading disorder and a written language disorder.

Jason, Grade 10

STUDENT PROFILES

Just think about what you know today. You read. You write. You work with numbers. You solve problems. We take all these things for granted. But of course you haven't always read. You haven't always known how to write. You weren't born knowing how to subtract 199 from 600. Someone showed you. There was a moment when you moved from not knowing to knowing, from not understanding to understanding. That's why I became a teacher.

- Phillip Done, educator and author

In Their Own Words
Students with LBLD Talk about School

There is nothing easy about writing.

Tomas, age 7

I know what I want to say but sometimes it doesn't come out right.

Aleesha, age 11

Even when I know a lot of information about something, when I have to talk about it or write it down, it gets confusing and I forget to include things. It is really frustrating when people don't understand what I'm saying and I get bad grades.

James, age 14

I have a lot of great ideas for my writing, but it is hard to organize my thoughts and putting the sentences together. One thing that really helps is using templates and reading it out loud .

Katrina, age 17

WHAT TO DO

While all student writers make errors and show room for improvement, oral and written language samples from students with unremediated language deficits often stand out. They are notable for many errors, often in more than one facet of language. Categorizing students' language strengths and errors provides the information needed to help students improve their skills.

Informal Language Diagnostics

We must know the challenges that students face when they listen, speak, read, and write if we are to facilitate effective skills instruction. Using the informal language diagnostic below, we can view students' written work from the perspective of language proficiency rather than content knowledge. Implementing the diagnostic is straightforward.

Online Resource Available

1. Provide two or three writing prompts from which students may choose.

2. Ask students to write down their names and the prompt they selected.

3. Give students 10 minutes to generate their best written response.

4. Collect the responses.

After collecting responses, categorize students' errors and strengths on the blank form provided in this chapter, or print one out at www.landmarkoutreach.org/lbld-resources. When you open this page, enter the username **(lbld)** and the password **(OUTREACH)**.

Use the information in figure 3 of chapter 2 to guide error categorization. The diagnostic may be used for oral or written language. When using the diagnostic for oral language, the boxes for prosody and pragmatics also need to be completed.

Why Informal Diagnostics Support Effective Instruction

Some writing errors may fall into more than one category. For instance, if a student writes *barf* for *bark*, it is most commonly marked as a spelling error without other differentiation. However, the error falls into both the phonological and semantic categories. In terms of phonology, it shows that the student heard the final sound as /f/ rather than /k/ and wrote what she heard. In terms of semantics, the word changes the meaning of the sentence. *The dog began to barf,* is quite different from *The dog began to bark.* As a student's error patterns emerge, instruction can be tailored to address the particular weakness.

In writing sample 1 shown in figure 4, the student wrote *condender* for *contender*, showing that she heard /d/ rather than /t/. Alone, this error might not indicate a weakness in phonological processing, but when a pattern emerges it should raise concern. For instance, all of the spelling errors in writing sample 1 point to weak phonological processing. It is important to categorize student errors carefully, as the profile that emerges should offer rich information to guide future instruction.

Writing Samples

Two writing samples by high school students appear below, each followed by a completed sample diagnostic. Both writing samples are by students with LBLD and so illustrate the unique language needs of students who share a diagnosis. While both writing samples have multiple errors in the syntax category, the points made by the first writer are not as clearly stated as those made by the second writer. So, too, the weaknesses in discourse the first writer demonstrates are not apparent in the second writing sample. Why? The first writer has an expressive language disorder in addition to dyslexia, while the second writer has dyslexia only.

Informal Language Diagnostic Example 1

The first writing sample (figure 4) is by a 10th-grade girl with an expressive language disorder and dyslexia. The sample is her 10-minute response to a prompt to write about violence in the media. A completed informal language diagnostic for this writing sample follows.

> Hollywood, A place were alot of
> Student want to go, be and live.
> Hollywood Seem to atract alot
> Of Kids and teens to be like then
> What ever, movie that comes out
> and it has violence, people tend
> to Copy, Power rangers. the
> movie condender Seem to have
> Some act of violence and by
> Us whatching it and Copying
> it Seems to get us I more
> troble For Eample the movie
> Saw an act of Violence, But there
> is that one person who would
> want to try that to see If its
> real and If the become addictec
> to It will be a daliy thing
> WE copy everytning WE
> See on tv. Why? No one
> NOSES.

Figure 4. Writing sample 1 from a 10th-grade girl with expressive language disorder and dyslexia.

INFORMAL LANGUAGE DIAGNOSTIC

Language Facet	Examples from Student's Work *What Student Wrote*/What Student Meant
Phonology	*the*/they; *student*/students; *were*/where; *condender*/contender; *troble*/trouble; *eample*/example; *noses*/knows; *I*/in
Morphology	*seem*/seems; *student*/students
Semantics	*noses*/knows

Syntax	• *Hollywood. A place were a lot of student want to go, be and live.*
	
	  Hollywood is a place where a lot of students want to go, be, and live.
	
	• *Hollywood seem to atract a lot of kids and teens to be like them.*
	
	  Hollywood seems to attract a lot of kids and teens who want to be like the movie stars.
	
	• *What ever, movie that comes out and it has violence people tend to copy, powerrangers.*
	
	  Whatever violent movie comes out, people tend to copy the violence.
	
	• *the movie condender seem to have some act of violence and by us whatching it and copying it seems to get us I more troble…*
	
	  The movie, <u>The Contender</u>, portrays acts of violence. If people copy it, they will get in trouble.
	
	• *For Eample the movie saw an act of violence, But there is that one person who would want to try that to see If its real and If the become addicted to It will be a daliy thing*
	
	  For example, the movie shows an act of violence, but if a person decides to try it in real life, he or she may start to be violent on a daily basis.

Lexicon	Some vague language (a lot, thing)
Discourse	• Topic not clear until third sentence • Clear point intended despite the syntax. (What ever, movie that comes out and it has violence people tend to copy.) • Offers supporting examples, but the points are totally unclear because they're not specific (… *For Eample the move saw an act of violence but there is that one person…*") • Makes same point three times using slightly different words • Uses some transition words • Has a clear concluding sentence, but overgeneralizes the point about movies and violence made in the topic sentence

Prosody	NA
Pragmatics	NA
Other	**Additional Comments on Student's Work**
Capitalization	None on titles: *I*/in; *the*/The; *Eample*/example; *But*/but; *If*/if; *It*/it; *WE*/we; *tv*/TV; *NOSES*/knows
Punctuation	*its*/it's; periods and commas used with some understanding of rules in place but no consistent application
Spelling	*alot*/a lot; *atract*/attract; *what ever*/whatever; *whatching*/watching; *daliy*/daily
Legibility	Handwriting clear and spacing good

Informal Language Diagnostic Example II

The second writing sample (figure 5) is by an 11th-grade boy with dyslexia. The sample is his 10-minute response to a prompt to describe how it would feel to attend boarding school. A completed informal language diagnostic for this writing sample follows.

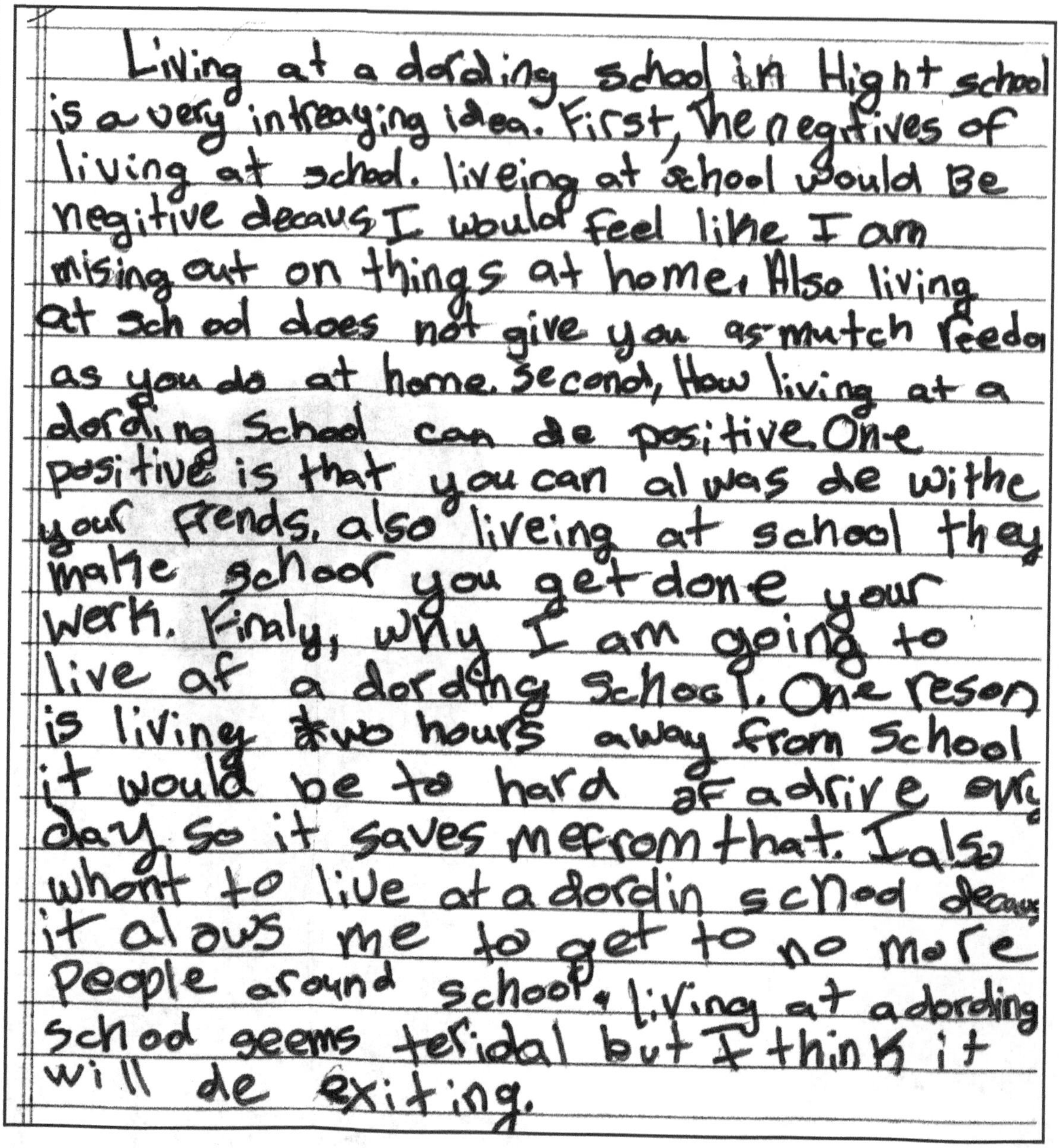

Living at a dording school im Hight school is a very intraying idea. First, the negitives of living at school. liveing at school would be negitive deaus I would feel like I am mising out on things at home. Also living at school does not give you as mutch feeda as you do at home. Second, How living at a dording school can de positive. One positive is that you can al was de with your frends. also liveing at school they make schoor you get done your werk. Finaly, why I am going to live at a dording school. One reson is living two hours away from school it would be to hard af a drive evry day so it saves me from that. I also whont to live at a dordin schod deaus it alows me to get to no more people around school. living at a dording schod seems teridal but I think it will de exiting.

Figure 5. Writing sample 2 from an 11th-grade boy with dyslexia.

Language Facet	Examples from Student's Work *What Student Wrote/What Student Meant*
Phonology	b/d reversals—*dording*/boarding; *teridal*/terrible; *decaus*/because Other: *Hight*/high; *reedom*/freedom
Morphology	NA
Semantics	• *to*/too; *no*/know • *... does not give you as mutch reedom as you <u>do</u> at home* 　...does not give you as much freedom as you <u>have</u> at home
Syntax	• Includes simple, compound, and complex sentence structures • Changes verb tense from conditional to present • Some sentences incomplete: *First, The negitives of living at school.* 　First, there are negatives to living at school. *Second, How living at a dording school can de positive.* 　Second, living at a boarding school can be positive. *Finaly, why I am going to live af a dording school.* 　Finally, there are a few reasons why I am going to live at a boarding school. • Some issues with sequence and efficient word order: *also liveing at school they make schoor you get done your werk.* 　Also, when you live at school they make sure you get your work done. *One reson is living two hours away from school it would be to hard of a drive evry day so it saves me from that.* 　One good reason to live at school is to save myself from a daily two-hour drive each way.
Lexicon	Language is specific; a few descriptive words included (intriguing, terrible, exciting)
Discourse	• Clear topic in first sentence that is developed throughout the composition with subtopics (negatives, positives, and reasons) • Each subtopic is supported by two examples • Clear concluding sentence • Use of transition words (first, also, second, finally)

INFORMAL LANGUGE DIAGNOSTIC

INFORMAL LANGUAGE DIAGNOSTIC

Prosody	NA
Pragmatics	NA
Other	**Additional Comments on Student's Work**
Capitalization	Capitalization not consistent *Hight school*/high school; *First, The*/First, the; *Second, How*/Second, how; *with your Friends*/with your friends; *living*/Living; …
Punctuation	Understands periods and use of commas after an introductory word, though doesn't apply consistently. Does not add comma into either of the two compound sentences.
Spelling	NOTE: many reversals of b/d in addition to other spelling errors. *dording*/boarding; *Hight*/high; *intreaging*/intriguing; negitives/negatives; liveing/living; negitive/negative; decaus/because; mising/missing; mutch/much; reedom/freedom; dording/boarding; de/be; alwas/always; de/be; withe/with; frends/friends; liveing/living; schoor/sure; werk/work; Finaly/Finally; af/at; dording/boarding; reson/reason; to/too; evry/every; whont/want; dordin/boarding; decaus/because; alows/allows; no/know; dording/boarding; teridal/terrible; de/be; exiting/exciting
Legibility	Handwriting legible; spacing fine though a bit crowded

Language Facet	Examples from Student's Work *What Student Wrote/What Student Meant*
Phonology	
Morphology	
Semantics	
Syntax	

INFORMAL LANGUGE DIAGNOSTIC

INFORMAL LANGUAGE DIAGNOSTIC

Discourse	
Prosody (Speaking)	
Pragmatics (Speaking)	
Other	**Additional Comments on Student's Work**
Capitalization	
Punctuation	
Spelling	
Legibility	

Chapter 3
Academic Skill Areas Affected by LBLD

WHAT TO KNOW

The relationship between language proficiency and academic success is direct. Language skills are necessary for literacy, and literacy is an essential element of academic proficiency. The paragraphs below offer an overview of how a language-based learning disability can affect the development of academic skills.

Reading

Reading consists of two related but discrete components: decoding automaticity and comprehension. *Decoding automaticity* is the ability to recognize and read words quickly and accurately. *Comprehension* is the ability to make meaning from the words. *Reading fluency* is the combined effect of automaticity and comprehension. It is the ability to read written language quickly, accurately, and with appropriate phrasing and expression (prosody) in order to grasp meaning (comprehend).

Decoding Automaticity

The most prevalent LBLD is a reading disorder. *Dyslexia* exists when the student's primary difficulty is decoding written text. Most students with dyslexia have difficulty processing language at the phonemic and morphemic levels. Their hearing acuity is fine, but they process sounds differently, which makes speedy, accurate decoding difficult. Often, these students are diagnosed

> Reading fluency is the combined effect of automaticity and comprehension. It is the ability to read written language quickly, accurately, and with appropriate phrasing and expression (prosody) in order to grasp meaning (comprehend).

with a *phonological processing disorder*. Other students' poorly developed reading skills result from differences in visual processing, which interferes with developing reading automaticity. These students may be diagnosed with a *visual processing disorder*.

In addition to interfering with the development of decoding automaticity, both phonological and visual processing differences impede spelling skills. These challenges lead students to difficulties with reading comprehension and writing skills.

Reading Comprehension

Reading comprehension difficulties are generally secondary to other challenges with language. Some students have difficulty decoding written text and may misread important words and misunderstand information. Other students may read so slowly or work so hard at sounding out words that the meaning gets lost. Either group probably could comprehend the text were it read aloud. On the other hand, students with limited vocabulary or a diminished understanding of syntax (the case for students diagnosed with mixed receptive-expressive language disorder) may have no difficulty decoding text quickly and accurately, but tremendous difficulty comprehending what they read or what has been read to them.

While many students with LBLD develop neither automaticity nor fluency without direct, intensive intervention, some manage to develop enough reading skill to get to middle and even high school without parents or teachers becoming aware of their weak skills. The difficulty is revealed when the volume and complexity of the reading become too challenging for students to keep up without help.

Writing

Writing involves both fine motor skills and two discrete yet related language skills: spelling (*orthography*) and expressive language. A fluent writer can spell and express an idea in writing coherently. Fluent spelling reflects mastery of the phonemic, morphemic, and semantic facets of language. Fluent written expression reflects spelling skill plus mastery of syntax within an appropriate discourse structure. Difficulty with any facet of language, from phonemes to discourse, can impede the development of fluent writing skills.

Language-based writing difficulties generally coincide with challenges in other areas of language. Students who struggle with decoding may also struggle with spelling. Students who struggle with spoken language are likely to produce writing with limited vocabulary, confused sentence structure, too much or too little information, or a disorganized argument or narrative. These difficulties may result from an expressive language disorder (characterized by difficulty producing learned language) or a mixed receptive-expressive language disorder (characterized by difficulty acquiring and producing language). Listening to and observing students as they speak and write can highlight the locus of a particular student's difficulty, especially in conjunction with formal evaluations.

Most students with LBLD need explicit, intensive, individualized instruction to develop spelling and writing skills. As with reading, however, some develop enough skills to get by until they become overwhelmed by the intensive demands of writing as they move through middle school and into high school.

Note that some students have difficulty writing because of poorly developed fine motor and visual-spatial skills. They have difficulty writing neatly, typing quickly, and organizing words on a page clearly. Though such difficulties frequently coexist with a language-based difficulty, they are not language-based in themselves and require different interventions.

Listening and Speaking

Whereas reading and writing must be explicitly taught to all children, oral language skills (listening and speaking) generally develop naturally and in relatively predictable patterns as infants and young children are exposed to them.

> Difficulty with any facet of language, from phonemes to discourse, can impede the development of fluent writing skills.

> Because reading and writing skills develop in relation to listening and speaking skills, difficulty developing any one skill area can impede a student's progress in others. Interventions need to address the full range of a student's difficulties.

Receptive Language

Receptive language skills enable us to comprehend spoken and written words and sentences, as well as nonverbal communication. Underdeveloped skills in this area make it difficult to process and remember spoken and written language in spite of intact hearing and visual acuity. Students may misunderstand words, sentences, and more complex information, as well as nonverbal information from body language or pictures and diagrams. As a result, both classroom learning and social interaction pose tremendous challenges.

Expressive Language

Expressive language skills enable us to speak and write clearly, meaningfully, and efficiently. Because these skills depend on receptive language skills, students with receptive difficulties also exhibit expressive difficulties. Some students who comprehend language may have difficulty using it. Limited speech, lack of specific language, word-finding difficulty, talking too little or too much, difficulty making a point, omissions of critical parts of sentences, and unusual syntax are examples of expressive language difficulty. Often, students who struggle with expressive language skills cannot express what they know unless they learn specific strategies for producing effective communication.

As with reading and writing, some students will not exhibit significant weaknesses until the increasing language demands of school exceed the strategies they developed to get by in previous years. Students with a language-based learning disability that involves receptive or expressive language skills require early, direct, intensive, and individualized intervention. Because reading and writing skills develop in relation to listening and speaking skills, difficulty developing any one skill area can impede a student's progress in others. Interventions need to address the full range of a student's difficulties.

Mathematics

Math proficiency requires more than calculating answers. It involves problem-solving, communicating mathematical concepts, reasoning and establishing proof, and representing information in different forms (PBS, 2002). Many of these skills require not only facility with numerical reasoning, but also oral and written language fluency. Weak language proficiency can therefore impede progress in math. Students may have difficulty processing oral directions, decoding written directions or word problems, reading or writing equations, or explaining their problem-solving process in words. While their number sense, arithmetic, and even mathematical thinking may be solid, their weaknesses in language interfere with their ability to learn and demonstrate mathematical knowledge.

Other students who demonstrate proficient language skills but struggle with math may have a math disability – sometimes called *dyscalculia*. Mathematics difficulties can occur for a variety of reasons and can emerge at any time during a student's schooling. As with difficulties acquiring language and literacy skills, students who do not receive appropriate instruction to address their math difficulties may avoid math and fall further behind their peers as they move through school.

> A lack of language proficiency can impede progress in math.

STUDENT PROFILES

STUDENT PROFILES

The student profiles section of each chapter introduces different facets of five students: Lan, Carlos, Ayanna, Elijah, and Jason. Each experiences difficulties in school that teachers must analyze and address. The profiles are composites of several actual students whose names have been changed here.

Students have unique learning profiles that reflect their educational experience, their learning, thinking, and personality styles, and their particular areas of need for language acquisition and use. All students who struggle in school - particularly those with LBLD - benefit from structured, multisensory, skills-based instruction. Each requires individualized instruction targeted at his or her specific needs. The student profiles in this book are included to encourage teachers' thinking about students in their own classes.

Language-Based Interventions

As you read about the language-based interventions for each student, keep in mind the following questions:

WHAT ARE SOME OF THE PROS AND CONS OF THE LANGUAGE-BASED INTERVENTIONS DESCRIBED?

WHAT QUESTIONS WOULD YOU WANT ANSWERED ABOUT EACH STUDENT'S PROGRAM IF YOU WERE THAT STUDENT?

WHAT QUESTIONS WOULD YOU WANT ANSWERED ABOUT EACH STUDENT'S PROGRAM IF YOU WERE THE PARENT OF THE STUDENT?

Also think about your own students:

WHAT LANGUAGE-BASED INTERVENTIONS DO YOU USE?

HOW DO YOU MATCH THE INTERVENTION TO THE STUDENT?

WHAT TOOLS DO YOU USE TO MEASURE STUDENT PROGRESS?

Lan, Grade 2

As a result of diagnostic assessment, LAN has had several interventions and progress assessment plans instituted. She is now in her school's language-based program. Part of the curriculum is an intensive program to remediate Lan's phonological processing disorder and a remedial language class focused on strategies for organizing oral and written language. In addition, a counselor and Lan's teachers coach her in strategies for managing her frustration and communicating her thoughts to others. Lan's content area teachers, with the help of special educators, provide her with the support she needs to read grade-level content material and the structure and cues she needs to express her knowledge.

Carlos, Grade 4

CARLOS started on new medication, which caused some problems and required adjustment several times. Now, Carlos, his teachers, and his parents report that he is more alert and less impulsive with his schoolwork. In response to his self-reports about his difficulties, Carlos began attending an after-school homework club where he completes his work in a quiet space under a teacher's supervision and can leave it in his desk to turn in the next day. In addition, Carlos's teacher agreed to try two changes. First, she began providing an example for all written assignments and projects, as well as step-by-step instructions for students to follow. Second, she started to check students' assignment folders to ensure they wrote down their homework.

Ayanna, Grade 6

AYANNA was placed in a self-contained language-based classroom for middle school students, where she receives intensive instruction in language skills. Though she has made some progress, her teachers remain concerned. Outside specialists were consulted and highlighted that while Ayanna has a language-based learning disability like the other students in the class, her profile is very different. She has below-average scores on tests of cognitive ability and limited language acquisition in both English and Hindi, her native language. Ayanna, and others like her, need the same instructional approaches as other students with LBLD, but they need it more intensively and for a longer period. Ayanna and two of her classmates now receive daily sessions in vocabulary development, sentence construction and manipulation for oral and written expression, and reading comprehension strategies, using texts that are accessible given their level of language development.

STUDENT PROFILES

ELIJAH'S courses now take place within an inclusionary language-based program at his middle school. In this program, students with and without learning disabilities work together in classes facilitated by a content teacher and a special educator. All teachers use the same vocabulary to instruct students in listening, speaking, reading, writing, and study skills, and they implement consistent teaching strategies across the classes. In addition to these courses, Elijah takes a second language arts class that is specially designed to help students with expressive language difficulties. In the class, students learn and practice strategies to recall and organize language for oral and written expression.

Elijah, Grade 8

JASON was given access to digitized versions of his school texts and assigned to a daily resource room for reading and writing instruction. Over a period of months, and with increasing time in the resource room, Jason made progress but began to miss school days and talk more about dropping out to pursue his landscaping business with his brother. His performance on the school's standardized assessment system (a predictor of state assessment performance) was still in the failing range in language arts. After a full educational evaluation, the recommendation was that Jason receive intensive, individualized tutoring to remediate his reading and written language disorder. He now attends daily tutoring sessions with two other students to remediate deficits in phonological processing. He also moved to a language-arts class taught by a former special education teacher.

Jason, Grade 10

Never compare one student's test score to another's. Always measure a child's progress against her past performance. There will always be a better reader, mathematician, or baseball player. Our goal is to help each student become as special as she can be as an individual--not to be more special than the kid sitting next to her.
- Rafe Esquith, educator and author

In Their Own Words
Students with LBLD Talk about School

Super long words are hard for me to read. It's easier for me to read when there aren't as many letters. Concentrating is hard because a lot of people talk.

Ali, age 7

When I read my eyes skip lines without my noticing so it's hard to understand.

Emory, age 12

Writing is pretty easy when I have a computer. The only real trouble I have is that sometimes I have too many ideas.

Mikael, age 13

One of the hardest things is listening to lectures and following class discussions. When I don't understand it I stop listening and think about something else. It helps a lot if the teacher gets the students involved or asks us questions.

May, age 16

WHAT TO DO

Language and Literacy Checklists

The checklists in this section focus on specific concerns about students' language and literacy development. Specifying students' areas of difficulty (e.g., *constructing sentences with clear syntax* rather than just *writing*) gives us language to use with parents, evaluators, and students and guides our instruction.

The checklists that follow can be used with the other informal diagnostic instruments provided in this book to help guide decisions about Response to Intervention (RTI) and tiered instruction. They should not take the place of formal educational evaluations. The checklists can be photocopied and used as they appear here. They are also available online for printing or customizing at www. landmarkoutreach.org/lbld-resources. When you open this page, enter the username (**lbld**) and the password (**OUTREACH**).

Online Resource Available

AREAS OF DIFFICULTY CHECKLISTS

Reading Difficulty Checklist
Informal Diagnostic Inventory

Student Name: Date:

	Has difficulty naming and/or remembering letters
	Has difficulty blending sounds into words
	Has difficulty manipulating sounds within words
	Has trouble recognizing or making rhymes
	Confuses similar letters (d/p; p/q)
	Adds, omits, or transposes sounds in words (friends/friend; progess/progress; beard/bread)
	Confuses visually similar words (supper/slipper)
	Has difficulty recognizing sight words
	Tires easily while reading
	Loses place while reading
	Reads slowly
	Guesses at words while reading
	Substitutes or eliminates words while reading
	Adds or omits parts of words while reading
	Reads without expression
	Reads without recognizing punctuation
	Exhibits weak comprehension of information or ideas read
	Avoids or dislikes reading

Teacher Comments:

Writing Difficulty Checklist
Informal Diagnostic Inventory

Student Name: _____   Date: _____

	Makes many cross-outs or erasures
	Has difficulty forming shapes of letters and numbers
	Uses unusual pencil/pen grip
	Copies inaccurately
	Has difficulty starting to write or knowing what to write about
	Tires easily while writing
	Does not use punctuation accurately or consistently
	Writes incomplete or confusing sentences
	Spells poorly or inconsistently
	Has difficulty maintaining a topic
	Organizes information or ideas poorly(no main point, off topic, illogical order)
	Has difficulty elaborating on ideas
	Has difficulty with or avoids editing and proofreading
	Avoids or dislikes writing tasks

Teacher Comments:

AREAS OF DIFFICULTY CHECKLISTS

Listening and Speaking Difficulty Checklist
Informal Diagnostic Inventory

Student Name: Date:

	Has history of delays in learning to speak
	Speaks too quietly or loudly
	Exhibits halting speech (many pauses or delays in responding)
	Overuses verbal fillers (*um, you know, ah*)
	Mispronounces and/or confuses of words that sound similar, and uses malapropisms (*prickle* for *pickle, pay the troll* instead of *pay the toll*)
	Has difficulty rhyming
	Shows difficulty finding a name or word when speaking
	Uses limited vocabulary
	Frequently uses vague language (that *thing*, your *stuff*)
	Frequently misunderstands oral instructions
	Frequently requests repetition of oral information
	Has difficulty retelling a story
	Has difficulty repeating information that was just said
	Has difficulty maintaining a topic in conversation (convoluted narrative, sudden topic changes)
	Has difficulty elaborating on an idea
	Gives limited responses to questions (partial answers or single-word answers)
	Shows little interest in or avoidance of books or stories when read aloud
	Lacks understanding of colloquialisms (*What's up?*), puns, humor, and idiomatic language (in native language and in second language if fluent)
	Shows general difficulty with social communication skills: understanding the relationship between speaker and listener; interpreting tone of voice, facial expressions, and body language; beginning and ending a conversation; interrupting
	Talks excessively
	Seems unusually quiet

Teacher Comments:

Mathematics Difficulty Checklist
Informal Diagnostic Inventory

Student Name: Date:

	Demonstrates poor understanding of one-to-one correspondence
	Makes errors sequencing numbers, steps, and the like
	Has difficulty estimating or predicting answers
	Has difficulty recognizing patterns or making comparisons
	Lacks fluency with number facts (speed and accuracy)
	Demonstrates difficulty learning to tell time on an analog clock
	Makes frequent computational errors
	Exhibits poor mastery of the language of mathematics
	Has difficulty transitioning between numerical and verbal representations
	Shows poor understanding of the relationships between operations (addition/subtraction, multiplication/division)
	Has difficulty learning formulas and rules and when to apply them
	Has difficulty interpreting graphs and charts
	Poorly organizes written work (columns of numbers out of alignment)
	Avoids or appears to dislike math

Teacher Comments:

AREAS OF DIFFICULTY CHECKLISTS

...the calling of the teacher. There is no craft more privileged. To awaken in another human being powers, dreams beyond one's own; to induce in others a love for that which one loves; to make of one's inward present their future; that is a threefold adventure like no other.

- George Steiner, educator and author

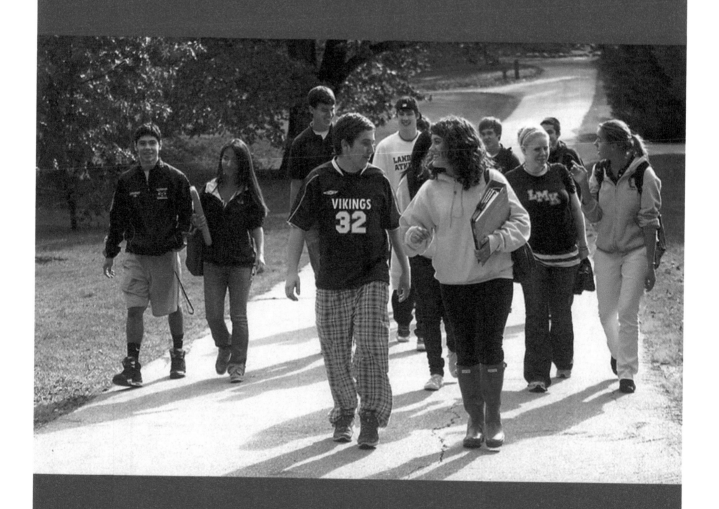

Chapter 4
Commonly Co-existing Difficulties

What to Know

Language-based difficulties can be complicated or exacerbated by other difficulties, such as weak executive function, motor disorders, or emotional issues. It is challenging for anyone, even neuropsychologists skilled in diagnostic assessment, to identify the range of difficulties affecting a student's academic performance and the most appropriate type and frequency of instruction needed. For classroom teachers, the first steps are to understand the possible roots of students' difficulties and to acknowledge that asking students to try harder or spend more time on their work will not move them toward academic proficiency.

Attention and Executive Function

Attention is the ability to focus on a stimulus long enough for it to reach consciousness. Focused attention is essential to all learning. Students with attentional difficulties pay attention, but often to too many things simultaneously. Their working memory becomes overwhelmed, making it difficult for them to sustain goal-oriented behavior and self-monitor for progress.

Students with attention difficulties are often diagnosed with one of three subtypes of *attention deficit hyperactivity disorder* (ADHD).

- The hyperactive/impulsive subtype includes difficulty inhibiting motor activity, including talking.

> Individuals with attention deficits or weak executive function usually can focus and sustain effort on a task of intense interest but struggle when they need to marshal these skills for school or other life activities.

- The inattentive type includes difficulty initiating and sustaining focus.

- The combined type includes significant difficulties with hyperactivity/impulsivity and inattention.

None of these diagnoses is a language-based difficulty, but all affect the acquisition and fluent use of language. All interfere with academic progress.

Executive function is the management system of the brain. Because attention is a central element in executive function, *executive function disorder* is increasingly cited in diagnostic evaluations even as it is not an official diagnostic category. Research in neuroscience is offering persuasive evidence for expanding existing definitions of ADD/ADHD to include executive function. Thomas E. Brown of Yale University proposes a model of ADD as primarily a problem with executive function. He writes:

> Although ADD/ADHD has been recognized for over 100 years, it has usually been seen as essentially a behavior problem. Yet many with ADD/ADHD suffer not from behavior problems so much as from chronic problems with focusing their attention, organizing their work, sustaining their effort, and utilizing short-term memory. (n.d., para. 1)

Unlike language difficulties, which are fairly consistent in how they manifest in each student, attention and executive function difficulties are variable. Educators often misinterpret this variability as evidence that a student is lazy. *He can spend hours building a LEGO castle, designing a Web site, or writing a play, but he doesn't finish his homework.* Laziness is simply inaccurate. Individuals with ADHD/weak executive function usually can focus and sustain effort on a task of intense interest but struggle when they need to marshall these skills for school or other life activities.

In fact, "The single most consistent finding across children who exhibit executive function difficulties of one type or another is the inconsistent nature of their behavior and/or academic production (McCloskey, Perkins, & Van Divner, 2008, p. 249).

Motor Skills

Gross motor skills are for large, generalized movements, such as running, kicking a ball, jumping rope, and riding a bike. *Fine motor skills* are for small, precise movements, such as beading, manipulating small blocks, using scissors, drawing, and writing. *Motor disorders* are not language-based, but many students with LBLD experience them. Difficulties with gross motor skills can profoundly affect students' social experience in school, but generally do not interfere with academics. Difficulties with fine motor skills affect both.

Fine motor skills are essential to many aspects of classroom learning. They affect handwriting and, sometimes, keyboarding. Students need to be fluent in one or both to write assignments, take notes, and answer questions on quizzes and tests. Students may struggle with building and other hands-on activities. Younger students are expected to construct bridges from toothpicks, create dioramas, make posters, and illustrate stories. Older students are expected to perform dissections, measure and mix chemicals, construct models, and use mathematical instruments. Outside the classroom, weak fine motor skills may stop students from tying their shoes on the fly, using a game controller, whittling a stick, making a friendship bracelet, and peeling an orange. Such difficulties can create feelings of inadequacy and bring on teasing from peers.

Motor disorders are not language-based, but many students with LBLD experience them.

Social and Emotional Adjustment

All students experience social and emotional difficulty at some point in their school career. For some, these difficulties are themselves disabling. Social and emotional adjustment is perhaps the

> Some students' school difficulties *indirectly result* from poor social skills, behavior problems, or emotional disturbances... Other students' school difficulties *are directly caused* by poor social skills, behavior problems, or emotional disturbances.

most complex of the topics addressed in this chapter, partly because of the breadth and depth of the difficulties, and partly because sorting out their causes and effects can be challenging. Difficulties with social and emotional adjustment can cause academic difficulty, or result from it.

Some students' academic difficulties are caused by poor social skills, behavior problems, or emotional disturbances. Students who are verbally combative, for example, may spend so much time in the hall, in detention, or suspended that their academic progress is affected. They fall behind, fail, lose motivation, and give up. Students who are severely depressed may struggle to find the energy to come to class, much less to complete homework or participate in a group project. They may not have a language-based learning disability, but their academic progress is impeded nonetheless and interventions are necessary.

Other students' exhibit poor social skills, behavior problems, or emotional disturbances as a result of their academic difficulties. Students with mixed receptive-expressive language disorder may have poor social skills because they lack sufficient language to understand and respond appropriately when interacting with others. Students with a reading disorder may disrupt class with inappropriate comments or actions to avoid reading in front of others or may become overwhelmed by an in-class reading assignment. Finally, students with all types of learning disabilities and differences commonly struggle with anxiety and depression resulting from their school difficulties. Poor school performance destroys their sense of self-efficacy. They are often accused of being lazy, stupid, dependent, stubborn, or troublesome. They may begin to believe these accusations themselves. When this occurs, it compounds the difficulties caused by the learning disability.

STUDENT PROFILES

The student profiles section of each chapter introduces different facets of five students: Lan, Carlos, Ayanna, Elijah, and Jason. Each experiences difficulties in school that teachers must analyze and address. The profiles are composites of several actual students whose names have been changed here.

Students have unique learning profiles that reflect their educational experience, their learning, thinking, and personality styles, and their particular areas of need for language acquisition and use. All students who struggle in school - particularly those with LBLD - benefit from structured, multisensory, skills-based instruction. Each requires individualized instruction targeted at his or her specific needs. The student profiles in this book are included to encourage teachers' thinking about students in their own classes.

Interventions for Other Difficulties

As you read about interventions for each student, keep in mind the following questions:

WHAT ISSUE(S) LIE AT THE CORE OF THE STUDENT'S DIFFICULTIES?

DO THE INTERVENTIONS SEEM SUFFICIENT? WHY OR WHY NOT?

WHAT ROLE WOULD YOU PLAY IN SUPPORTING EACH STUDENT?

Also think about your own students:

WHICH STUDENTS HAVE BEHAVIOR DIFFICULTIES? ATTENTION DIFFICULTIES? MOTOR SKILLS DIFFICULTIES? SOCIAL OR EMOTIONAL CHALLENGES?

ARE YOU AWARE OF THE CAUSE OF THESE DIFFICULTIES?

WHAT COULD YOU DO TO SUPPORT AND EMPOWER THESE STUDENTS?

LAN has difficulty with social and emotional adjustment. Because of her reading disorder, she often feels dumb and that her teachers and parents are disappointed in spite of her efforts to improve. These feelings lead to anger and frustration, so she responds negatively to instruction or suggestions or simply refuses to do what is asked of her. Because of her expressive language disorder, Lan has difficulty demonstrating her knowledge and skill. She has the vocabulary, but has difficulty using it efficiently. As a result, she is often misunderstood by her peers and adults, who think she talks too much, makes no sense, or just suddenly explodes. None of these interpretations of Lan's behavior are accurate.

Lan, Grade 2

ADHD and executive function weaknesses are the roots of CARLOS'S poor performance in school. With medication and some environmental changes, he is better able to sustain focus on academic tasks. With teacher modeling and explicit instruction, he can identify a goal, follow a map to achieve it, and monitor his work along the way. An added benefit is Carlos's improved confidence that he can be as good at schoolwork as he is at building robots. He just needs to learn the right strategies.

Carlos, Grade 4

In addition to AYANNA'S challenges with receptive and expressive language, she has a fine motor disorder and receives occupational therapy once a week. Ayanna's handwriting is legible but labored and oddly spaced on the page. Additionally, she has some difficulty folding and working with scissors, tweezers, and small parts. She finds these troubles embarassing when working cooperatively with other students. Ayanna is practicing her handwriting skills as well as learning keyboarding skills, which she missed in her other school due to pull-outs for reading tutoring.

Ayanna, Grade 6

In addition to ELIJAH'S challenges with expressive language, he has ADHD and struggles with a variety of social and emotional issues. In terms of his academic performance, a trial of medication for ADHD has been successful, particularly combined with participating in the school's language-based program and checking in daily with his advisor to help him stay organized and focused on short-term

Elijah, Grade 8

goals. Elijah's social and emotional difficulties result from a complicated background, however, and academic interventions are not enough to support him. Elijah meets weekly with a licensed social worker to develop strategies for communicating his feelings and needs, monitoring his behavior, and managing his anger. In addition, Elijah and his foster parents meet for counseling outside of school.

Jason, Grade 10

While JASON has difficulties with academics, his school and home life pose no unusual challenges. He is connected with his neighborhood and church communities, and he and his older brother have built a successful landscaping business. According to his mother and his guidance counselor, the biggest challenge is convincing him to postpone full-time landscaping work and complete high school.

STUDENT PROFILES

In Their Own Words
Students with LBLD Talk about School

People bugging me is the hard part. People are talking and I can't concentrate. It's easier for me when no one is talking.

Max, age 7

I get in trouble a lot.

Aleesha, age 10

I can't think straight when people are talking to me. People always expect you to listen AND take notes, or to do your math while everybody is talking. It's totally frustrating.

Emory, age 14

I have dyslexia. I have ADHD. I have asthma. I wear glasses. I'm kind of a klutz. I get anxious a lot. It's just who I am. Some stuff is hard for me, some of it's not. I think my life will be a lot better when I can take fewer classes at a time in college.

John, age 17

WHAT TO DO

Checklists for Other Difficulties

The checklists in this section focus on specific concerns about difficulties that commonly co-exist with students' LBLD.

Specifying students' areas of difficulty (e.g., difficulty remaining focused during class discussion rather than distractible) gives us language to use with parents, evaluators, counselors, and students and helps guide interventions.

The checklists that follow can be used with the other informal diagnostic instruments provided in this book to guide instructional decision-making. They should not take the place of formal educational or psychological evaluations. They are also available online for printing or customizing at www.landmarkoutreach.org/lbld-resources. When you open this page, enter the username (**lbld**) and the password (**OUTREACH**).

Online Resource Available

AREAS OF DIFFICULTY CHECKLISTS

Attention & Executive Function Difficulty Checklist
Informal Diagnostic Inventory

Student Name: Date:

	Easily loses focus on tasks when there are distractors
	Acts on impulse (does not stop to check answers or consider consequences of behavior)
	Makes mistakes in work in spite of knowledge or skill
	Has difficulty making transitions (to new schedules, to changed expectations)
	Has difficulty setting goals or making plans
	Has difficulty shifting from one task to another
	Resists shifting strategies to accomplish a task
	Has difficulty evaluating progress toward a goal
	Often performs tasks too quickly or too slowly
	Has difficulty initiating or completing required tasks
	Has difficulty sustaining focus or effort on required tasks
	Performs very inconsistently across subjects and tasks, and day to day
	Becomes easily frustrated or angered
	Gives up easily when challenged
	Tends to lose belongings
	Often forgets materials
	Avoids or dislikes certain tasks that require significant effort (procrastinates, makes excuses)
	Has difficulty sitting still (fidgets, taps, makes noises)
	Does not follow directions completely
	Frequently interrupts in conversations

Teacher Comments:

Motor Difficulties Checklist
Informal Diagnostic Inventory

Student Name:	Date:

	Uses unusual pencil/pen grip
	Maintains unusual posture while writing
	Has difficulty producing legible handwriting
	Has difficulty with fine motor tasks (zipping, buttoning, cutting)
	Performs fine motor tasks very slowly or only with great effort
	Frequently drops things
	Walks or runs with unusual gait
	Frequently trips, falls, or runs into things
	Has difficulty with gross motor tasks (carrying books, jumping rope, catching or throwing a ball, swinging on swings)

Teacher Comments:

AREAS OF DIFFICULTY CHECKLISTS

Social & Emotional Difficulty Checklist
Informal Diagnostic Inventory

AREAS OF DIFFICULTY CHECKLISTS

Student Name: Date:

	Seems unaware of or unresponsive to others' moods
	Has difficulty identifying or responding to good-natured teasing or humor
	Exhibits flat affect (does not often smile or frown; speech mostly demonstrates lack of emotion)
	Shows an extreme lack of energy
	Does not respond to others' prompts (greetings, questions)
	Has difficulty making a friend or joining or maintaining a peer group
	Has trouble expressing feelings or over-expresses feelings
	Talks too much or too little
	Has difficulty with self-control when frustrated or angry
	Is prone to tantrums or violent outbursts
	Overreacts to stimuli
	Has trouble adjusting to the unexpected
	Avoids identifying personal strengths and challenges
	Lacks confidence
	Shows poor sense of self-efficacy
	Seems anxious about or fearful of school or schoolwork
	Complains of difficulties eating or sleeping, or with general health
	Makes negative comments about self or others

Teacher Comments:

Chapter 5
Facilitating Success

WHAT TO KNOW

Children between the ages of 6 and 18 spend close to half their waking lives in school. During those years, parents, teachers, and peers deeply influence their lives. Students are at a profound disadvantage if they do not receive early and appropriate instruction to build the skill areas essential for success in school. It is equally important for adults to recognize students' academic potential and nurture their strengths. Research indicates that success for students with learning differences and disabilities depends not only on designing an effective program for academic success but equally on developing positive social and emotional environments both at home and in school.

Facilitating Academic Success

Many highly successful people experienced difficulty in school. An Internet search turns up scores of familiar names, including Nelson Rockefeller, Charles Schwab, Jay Leno, Danny Glover, Avi, and John Irving. Each of these people gained success in their adult lives.

Most success stories are less well known. Many thousands of people with learning disabilities finish school and build fulfilling careers, create families, and contribute to society in innumerable

> As classroom teachers, we can provide students with the feeling of self-efficacy that is essential for academic success in two key ways: by teaching them strategies to approach difficult academic tasks and by believing in their capacity to learn.

ways. Often, people with learning disabilities are particularly creative thinkers and visionary leaders. Some studies have found that individuals with language difficulty develop superior skills in other areas, such as art, music, dance, mechanics, cooking, and athletics. Additionally, much research has demonstrated that students whose difficulties are identified early and addressed with appropriate teaching can achieve academic levels equal or superior to peers without learning disabilities.

As classroom teachers, we can provide students with the feeling of self-efficacy that is essential for academic success in two key ways: by teaching them strategies to approach difficult academic tasks and by believing in their capacity to learn. Parker J. Palmer, author of *The Courage to Teach* (2007), offers this reminder:

> Students who learn are the finest fruit of teachers who teach . . . . I am also clear that in lecture halls, seminar rooms, field settings, labs, and even electronic classrooms – the places where most people receive most of their formal education – teachers possess the power to create conditions that can help students learn a great deal – or keep them from learning much at all. Teaching is the intentional act of creating those conditions, and good teaching requires that we understand the inner sources of both the intent and the act. (p. 6)

Landmark's Six Teaching Principles™

Landmark's Six Teaching Principles™ create the conditions for learning that students with learning disabilities need to succeed. Students with LBLD make stunning progress with targeted, intensive, skills-based instruction under these conditions. Essentially, these principles are:

- *Provide opportunities for success* to foster a sense of self-efficacy.

- *Use multisensory approaches* so that all content is conveyed in visual, auditory, and tactile modes (see it, hear it, say it, do something with it).

- *Micro-unit and structure tasks* to form step-by-step processes, which facilitate learning and provide incremental opportunities for success that help students persist in the face of longer, more complex tasks.

- *Ensure automatization through practice and review*, as consistency and repetition develop skill.

- *Provide models* to give students samples of successful work and set clear standards, which helps students begin assignments and self-assess as they work.

- *Include students in the learning process*, because increasing students' self-awareness as learners helps them engage and invest in the classroom.

> Students with LBLD make stunning progress with targeted, intensive, skills-based instruction that follows Landmark's Six Teaching Principles™.

The full text of Landmark's Six Teaching Principles™ is available at the front of this book.

Facilitating Social and Emotional Strengths

Successful people have high self-esteem because they accept their strengths and weaknesses as elements of who they are. They acknowledge what they are good at and have learned or developed a repertoire of effective strategies to cope with difficulty.

Unfortunately, too many students lack a strong support network that nurtures their strengths, facilitates self-awareness and self-advocacy skills, and teaches them strategies for coping with difficulty. They may be misunderstood and criticized for their weaknesses at home and experience frustration, anxiety, and failure at school. These are the students who may fail courses or drop out of school, get in trouble with the law, or engage in risky

> Unfortunately, too many students lack a strong support network that nurtures their strengths, facilitates self-awareness and self-advocacy skills, and teaches them strategies for coping with difficulty.

behavior because they lack a practical understanding of their competence and potential. Alternatively, these are the students who can be empowered by appropriate instruction and strengthened by others' belief in their ability to succeed.

A 20-year longitudinal study of people with learning disabilities who attended the Frostig Center (a school for students with learning disabilities in Pasadena, California) found that those who were most successful had developed an array of emotional and social attributes that predicted their success as adults better than tests of intelligence or academic achievement (Goldberg, Higgins, Raskind, & Herman, 2003; Raskind, Goldberg, Higgins, & Herman, 2002).

Howard Gardner's research and writing laid the groundwork for many children with LBLD to understand that having a learning disability does not mean they are stupid. In *Frames of Mind: The Theory of Multiple Intelligences* (1983), Gardner critiqued the notion that there is one human intelligence that can be measured by psychometric tests. Positing the existence of multiple intelligences (intelligences beyond those traditionally required for academic achievement, such as linguistic and mathematical intelligences), Gardner broadened our general understanding of what it means to be smart.

SOCIAL AND EMOTIONAL ATTRIBUTES FOR SUCCESS

SELF-AWARENESS

PROACTIVE RESPONSIVENESS TO CHALLENGES

ABILITY TO PERSEVERE

ABILITY TO SET GOALS

REPERTOIRE OF STRATEGIES FOR COPING WITH DIFFICULTY

USEFUL ACADEMIC SUPPORT SYSTEMS

POSITIVE FAMILY AND SOCIAL RELATIONSHIPS

In *Multiple Intelligences: New Horizons* (2006), Gardner extends his earlier work in relation to new developments in the field. When educators acknowledge and respond to the strengths and talents of students – particularly students who struggle with schoolwork – they empower them to accept their learning difficulties as challenges that are simply part of the unique and valuable individuals they are. Gardner is currently the senior director of Harvard University's Project Zero, whose research initiatives, in collaboration with schools, universities, and museums, "place the learner at the center of the educational process, respecting the different ways in which an individual learns at various stages of life, as well as differences among individuals in the ways they perceive the world and express their ideas" (Project Zero, 2010, para. 3).

GARDNER'S INTELLIGENCES

VERBAL/LINGUISTIC	BODILY/KINESTHETIC
LOGICAL/MATHEMATICAL	INTERPERSONAL
SPATIAL	INTRAPERSONAL
MUSICAL	NATURALISTIC/ ENVIRONMENTAL

> When educators acknowledge and respond to the strengths and talents of students – particularly students who struggle with schoolwork – they empower them to accept their learning difficulties as challenges that are simply part of the unique and valuable individuals they are.

Robert Brooks also reminds us of the importance of attending to more than academics. A member of Harvard University's School of Medicine faculty and former director of McLean's Hospital in Belmont, Massachusetts, Brooks is a writer and lecturer of national prominence. His work centers on developing resilience in young people. He is most often recognized for his mandate that adults carry the responsibility for helping children develop "islands of competence" – areas in which a child can excel and so develop a sense of being a capable, important human being. This metaphor developed in response to years of clinical practice in which he heard children, adolescents, and adults who seemed to be drowning in their self-perceived inadequacies. Brooks writes:

> This metaphor influenced the questions I posed and the strategies I initiated in my clinical practice. For example, whenever I meet with parents, teachers, or other professionals to discuss children who are burdened with problems, I ask them to describe the child's islands of competence. Next, I ask how we might strengthen these islands and display them for others to see. I have witnessed the ways in which these questions can alter the mindset of adults as they shift their energy from "fixing deficits" to "identifying and reinforcing strengths." (2005, para. 8)

The profound difference in this change in perspective – from fixing deficits to reinforcing strengths – has contributed to amazing success in the lives of many students who struggled in school.

STUDENT PROFILES

The student profiles section of each chapter introduce different facets of five students: Lan, Carlos, Ayanna, Elijah, and Jason. Each experiences difficulties in school that teachers must analyze and address. The profiles are composites of several actual students whose names have been changed here.

Students have unique learning profiles that reflect their educational experience, their learning, thinking, and personality styles, and their particular areas of need for language acquisition and use. All students who struggle in school - particularly those with LBLD - benefit from structured, multisensory, skills-based instruction. Each requires individualized instruction targeted at his or her specific needs. The student profiles in this book are included to encourage teachers' thinking about students in their own classes.

How to Facilitate Success

As you read about interventions for each student, keep in mind the following questions:

WHAT FACTORS HAVE CONTRIBUTED TO THE SUCCESS OF EACH STUDENT?

WHAT CAN BE DONE TO BUILD ON THE CURRENT SUCCESSES?

WHAT OTHER SUPPORTS OR INTERVENTIONS SHOULD BE PUT INTO PLACE FOR EACH STUDENT?

Also think about your own students:

WHICH STUDENTS SEEM NEGATIVE OR DISCOURAGED?

WHAT WILL I DO TO PROVIDE THEM WITH OPPORTUNITIES FOR SUCCESS?

STUDENT PROFILES

LAN is making good progress in her language-based program. Her negative emotional reactions to instruction have decreased substantially. The phonological processing intervention program appeals to her, and she receives positive feedback from her instructor. Lan's ability to organize written language has improved as well, thanks to her willing use of scaffolds for writing sentences. Her counselor reports that Lan notices a difference in the way her peers react to her now that she is using the communication strategies she is learning. Lan reports that she feels calmer now that she can see her progress and understand why teachers are trying to help her.

Lan, Grade 2

CARLOS is performing well in his classes. He is happy to finish his homework at school so he can get help if he needs it and is not distracted by his siblings at night. He says that having examples to look at helps him to picture what his work should look like at the end, "sort of the same way I picture my robots." He also feels the written instructions help him. "Before, Mr. S. used to just tell us what we were supposed to do, and I'd sort of space out and miss it. Now he gives us directions and shows us how to build our writing just like we'd build a building!" Mr. S. reports that he will continue using these teaching strategies because they are making a dramatic difference in almost all his students' work, not just those with LBLD.

Carlos, Grade 4

AYANNA is making good progress in her language-based classroom now that she is receiving additional instruction in vocabulary, sentence construction, and reading comprehension. She particularly enjoys choosing a book from her recommended reading list – a list of accessible books the teachers individualize for each student – for quiet reading time. Ayanna reports that she likes to read books now that she can understand what is happening. She expresses gratitude to her teachers because they know how to "make me learn right." Her teachers note that she has made several friends in the class, and her mother reports that she likes to read the books her teachers lend her.

Ayanna, Grade 6

Elijah, Grade 8

Elijah's progress in school has been dramatic. The expressive language strategies (particularly the use of oral rehearsal prior to writing and speaking) and scaffolds for managing language have empowered Elijah to demonstrate the depth of his knowledge in content areas. He reports a positive change overall, and especially appreciates having a required daily check-in with an advisor he likes. In his words: "I can't get away with stuff anymore. I'm kind of glad because I'm getting really good grades now."

Jason, Grade 10

Jason's reading began to improve dramatically after a month of daily tutoring. A half-year reading assessment showed his skills had increased to a seventh-grade level. He continues to use digital books to help him keep up in his content classes, and his grades have improved with that accommodation. His struggles with writing are ongoing, and he rarely volunteers to participate in class. He has been referred for a speech-language evaluation to determine the nature of his communication challenges.

STUDENT PROFILES

In Their Own Words
Students with LBLD Talk about School

My first grade teacher is my best teacher. She helps me write. It makes me happy.

Del, age 7

My mom is my best teacher. She teaches me a lot of things like cooking and how to fix things. She helps me with my homework every day after school. She thinks I'm smart.

Mira, age 10

I think my music teacher is the best teacher I have ever had. I study violin and piano. We listen to music, then she plays it to show me. Then I learn it a little at a time. We don't go too fast and she is really positive and enthusiastic. She is hard, but she helps me practice and I practice a lot on my own. I've gotten a lot better.

Sirina, age 12

Mr. H in third grade was the BEST teacher. He showed us exactly how to do stuff like lab reports and research papers. We did a real archaeological dig for artifacts! And we made books and a lot of other stuff. Most teachers just tell you to do things, but they don't teach you how. I had a hard time with math, but he pushed me in a really good way, and I accomplished the goal.

John, age 14

I don't really have a best teacher but in 9th grade I remember starting a school I hated. I wrote a personal essay for my English assignment, and the teacher said it was one of the funniest and best things she had ever read. It was the first time a teacher told me I was a good writer. Usually they just correct my spelling and grammar. It made me want to write more stories. I got really good at writing that year.

Robin, age 15

The best teacher I have had is my English teacher from 6th grade because she helped me get over my fear of talking in front of people. She made me feel confident in my presentations and myself.

Teebah, age 17

WHAT TO DO

Strategies to Help Students Succeed

The table in this section summarizes important things to know and do in order to help students find success. Hang it on a bulletin board. Pass it on to colleagues who are feeling discouraged about student performance. Share it with students so they can see that having learning difficulties really means they just need to be taught in a different way.

Also included in this section are lists of common interventions at different levels. These example accommodations and modifications are not intended to take the place of a full schedule of remedial instruction that builds skills for students with language-based learning disabilities and differences. They can, however, empower students to participate fully and successfully in classes with peers who do not share the same learning struggles.

Copies for download can be found at www.landmarkoutreach. org/lbld-resources. When you open this page, enter the username **(lbld)** and the password **(OUTREACH)**.

> **Online Resource Available**

FACILITATING SUCCESS

Ten Ways to Facilitate Success

	Know This	**Do This**
#1	Students with learning disabilities or differences are intelligent.	Recognize the strengths and talents poor grades often mask.
#2	Students with learning disabilities or differences want to succeed in school.	Talk with students about their strengths, plan how to address their needs with them, and believe in their potential.
#3	Students with learning disabilities or differences thrive in structured settings.	Be very organized and deliver structured lessons. Make performance expectations explicit through models, direction, and specific, supportive, individualized feedback throughout the process.
#4	Students with learning disabilities or differences want to know the purpose of their work.	Involve students in planning and goal-setting, and explicitly communicate objectives for content and assignments.
#5	Students with learning disabilities or differences are successful when they receive new information in multiple ways.	Provide abundant opportunities for students to process information and concepts. They need to hear it, see it, and do it so they can learn it.
#6	Students with learning disabilities or differences use their brains differently from other people and are often creative thinkers.	Offer choices and variety for how students can demonstrate their learning in class, on homework assignments, and through various forms of assessment designed to highlight different strengths.

#7	Students with learning disabilities or differences are motivated by success.	Provide every possible opportunity for successful performance. Share specific, positive feedback on what students do well.
#8	Students with learning disabilities or differences do not want to be singled out from other students.	Provide corrective feedback privately, and be tactful and subtle in providing accommodations.
#9	Students with learning disabilities or differences benefit from timely feedback on their performance.	Provide direct, specific answers to questions; immediate, logical responses to behavior; and fast feedback on assignments.
#10	Students with learning disabilities or differences are successful when they are surrounded by adults who believe in them.	Learn about students' learning disabilities or differences. Develop teaching skills to deliver class content in different ways. Be invested in helping students succeed.

Facilitating Success

FACILITATING SUCCESS

Common Accommodations to Support Language Comprehension and Expression

Talk with individuals about how they learn best, and try to accommodate their needs.

Monitor student's progress and make decisions about whether to continue, provide more, or change the accommodation(s).

Make the objectives of each lesson clear to students.

Provide models of expected work/behavior and discuss with students the elements of success (e.g., work samples, think-alouds, role-playing).

Explain information, concepts, and instructions using simple, clear sentences.

Present vocabulary, information, and concepts using a variety of multisensory methods.

Write key vocabulary, information, and concepts on the board.

Provide plentiful structured opportunities for students to engage in oral discussion; make sure all students have an opportunity to ask questions, offer comments, and respond to others' comments.

Provide phonemic, semantic, and gestural cues to aid language recall.

Provide sentence starters to spur language production (e.g., "The main character's weaknesses include…" or "Two examples of anti-war protests were…").

Wait extra time for processing before requiring verbal or behavioral responses; wait extra time for students to read and process prior to requiring a verbal or written response.

Ask follow-up questions to help students elaborate on their responses and provide examples to support their points.

Summarize or rephrase students' oral responses to check clarity and accuracy.

Ask students to rephrase information, concepts, and instructions they've heard or read.

Respond to questions specifically, and use different words when clarifying.

Teach students to use a small selection of graphic organizers to aid their language organization.

Teach students to use writing templates or scaffolds to structure their expressive language.

Provide audio books.

Allow the use of a computer (and voice activated software) for assignments.

Assess knowledge and skills in a variety of ways to ensure students have plenty of opportunity to use their strengths (e.g., oral examinations vs. written tests, visual projects that demonstrate mastery of content vs. essays).

Offer plenty of specific supportive feedback on students' efforts.

Discuss with students their personal goals and plans to achieve those goals.

Common Modifications to Support Language Comprehension and Expression

Talk with individuals and do informal assessments to determine specific areas of need.

Monitor the student's progress to determine whether to continue, provide more, or change the modifications.

Provide shortened readings and assignments.

Provide extra time and a quiet place for tests, and extra time to complete assignments.

Break longer or complex assignments into small parts, schedule due dates for the student, and check in on the student's progress on each step.

Identify the essential vocabulary, information, and concepts and ensure the student focuses on those, and is assessed only on those.

Provide texts that cover the same content but are written for lower reading levels (e.g., adapted novels, selected websites or texts that present the same concepts in simpler language).

Provide a daily summary or outline of the next day's lesson.

With the student, create notes that highlight important vocabulary and concepts for orally presented lessons, or provide partially completed notes the student can fill in during class.

With the student, create and practice using a guided reading protocol to aid reading comprehension.

Give the student advance notice about questions you will ask them so the student may prepare ahead of time.

Provide cues to prompt memory of newly learned vocabulary, information, and concepts.

Create structured activities that engage the student to interact with the language of the course (e.g., matching games, concept card sorting, collaborative activities that require discussion).

Set up a signal system that allows the student to communicate need for assistance silently.

Check student class work frequently to ensure understanding.

Schedule a daily end-of-class check-in for the student to summarize class and ask questions.

Assign "studying" that is active work (e.g., make flashcards, answer questions on a study guide).

Provide opportunities to re-do assignments if student did not understand expectations.

Provide opportunities for take-home tests, and opportunities for the student to demonstrate knowledge and skill through alternative assessments.

FACILITATING SUCCESS

FACILITATING SUCCESS

Examples of Remediation to Build Language Skills

Through assessment and observation, identify the specific area(s) requiring remediation.

Discuss with individuals their strengths and needs, the plans for remediation, and their progress in meeting established goals.

Set clear goals for progress, make a plan to build the skills to meet those goals, and provide highly structured, sequential, individualized instruction.

Provide remedial instruction individually or in small groups to students with similar skill levels and needs.

Do not neglect students' needs to access grade level content as they are able. Provide remediation to build language and literacy skills outside the general curriculum, but use accommodations and modifications in general education classes to enable students to build their content knowledge.

Provide instruction in vocabulary development/semantics. Practice identifying word meanings in reading selections and using newly learned language in speaking and writing.

Provide individualized instruction in phonological processing.

Provide individualized instruction in decoding and automaticity to develop reading fluency. Practice both oral and silent reading.

Provide individualized instruction in morphology. Practice new language skills through listening, speaking, reading and writing activities.

Provide individualized instruction in syntax. Practice new language skills through listening, speaking, reading and writing activities.

Teach discourse structures and their related cue words and phrases. Practice new language skills through listening, speaking, reading and writing activities.

Provide individualized instruction in prosody. Practice new language skills through listening, speaking, and oral reading.

Teach and practice interpreting and using pragmatic language (if this is a weakness).

Teach learning and study strategies explicitly, and practice frequently.

Observe the student's work in various settings to assess whether new skills are being generalized.

Carefully monitor student's progress in their areas of need to determine whether more or different interventions are needed.

Teach content-area teachers to incorporate parallel language skill-building into their curriculum and instruction.

Afterword

Many types of difficulties can interfere with students' academic progress. This book has addressed only a few of the most common. Good diagnostic assessments exist, as do many research-recommended interventions. Still, one classroom teacher cannot do everything. It is essential that schools build and strengthen teams whose purpose is to ensure that all students are making effective progress toward academic proficiency. It is equally important that teachers coach students as they develop the collaborative and interpersonal skills, self-efficacy, self-regulation, and emotional resiliency that provide the foundation for their success in higher education, the workplace, and the 21st century world in which they live.

In addition to a highly regarded professional development program, Landmark Outreach provides many resources in print and online to help teachers empower students. Please visit our website at www.landmarkout-reach.org to explore our offerings.

When our students fail, we, as teachers, too, have failed.
- Marva Collins, educator

We must not, in trying to think about how we can make a big difference, ignore the small daily differences we can make which, over time, add up to big differences that we often cannot foresee.
- Marian Wright Edelman, Children's Defense Fund founder

Glossary of Terms

ACADEMIC PROFICIENCY is the use and coordination of skills and strategies in order to demonstrate understanding of curriculum and perform at average or better levels on classroom and state assessments.

ADHD is an acronym for *attention deficit/hyperactivity disorder.* There are a variety of terms used to describe this disorder as the naming of it has changed with each successive publication of the Diagnostic Statistical Manual. Attention disorders are currently categorized into three subtypes: the inattentive type; the hyperactive type; and the combined type.

AUTOMATICITY is the ability to perform a task quickly and accurately with little or no conscious effort. In terms of reading, automaticity refers to immediate word recognition with no need to sound out the word phonetically.

DIAGNOSTIC ASSESSMENT is a category of assessment. Its purpose is to determine what difficulties a student is having and why. It can be formal (as in the tools used during neuropsychological, educational, speech-language, or behavioral evaluations) or informal (as in the analysis of specifically designed classroom assessments such as the informal language diagnostics in chapter 2).

DISCOURSE is the linking together of sentences to create purposeful and coherent communication of ideas. Discourse can be oral or written.

EDUCATIONAL EVALUATION refers to a series of diagnostic assessments and interviews with teachers, parents, and the student. Its purpose is to determine: what difficulties a student is experiencing; why; whether those difficulties are the result of a learning or other disability; and what educational interventions should be implemented to remediate the difficulties. An educational evaluation is similar to a neuropsychological evaluation, but is generally shorter in duration, assesses fewer areas of functioning, and is commonly carried out by a team that includes a psychologist, special education teacher(s), and other school specialists as needed.

EXECUTIVE FUNCTION is the coordination of cognitive and psychological processes that enable an individual to set goals, carry out a plan that achieves those goals, and self-monitor and shift approaches as needed.

EXPLICIT INSTRUCTION is a systematic approach to instruction that includes very high levels of teacher and student interaction and instructional principles that guide how content is selected and delivered. These principles include providing students with the big picture and purpose of the work; eliciting students' background knowledge; clear modeling, practicing of specific strategies and sharing feedback; scaffolding; guiding students' application of knowledge and strategies in varying contexts; and frequent individualized reviewing of material to ensure that previously learned content and strategies are retained, used, and built upon.

EXPRESSIVE LANGUAGE is a skill that enables an individual to communicate in language through speaking and writing. It develops in relation to receptive language, a skill that enables an individual to comprehend through listening and reading.

INTERNAL LANGUAGE refers to self-talk and self-questioning. All individuals use internal language to mediate sensory input. It is an essential component of executive function, as well as being important to self-efficacy and the comprehension and production of language. For example, people use internal language to motivate themselves when they're discouraged: "I know I can do this because I did it last week!" They use it to calm themselves: "I'm feeling sick because I'm nervous about my math test. I know if I breathe slowly and do the work carefully I'll be just fine." They use it to manage comprehension: "The teacher just said there were two villains in the story, but I only remember one. I need to go back and look at the story or ask the teacher about this."

LANGUAGE AND LITERACY SKILLS are terms used together in this book to underscore that listening and speaking skills provide the foundation for developing reading and writing skills. Often, schools use *literacy skills* in reference to reading and writing only. *Content literacy* and *disciplinary literacy* refer to understanding and using the vocabulary and patterns of thinking related to a specific academic discipline such as mathematics or history. *Language and literacy skills* are those required to comprehend and produce language including listening, speaking, reading, and writing.

LANGUAGE-BASED LEARNING DISABILITY (LBLD) refers to a spectrum of difficulties related to the understanding and use of spoken and written language. It falls under the umbrella of specific learning disability (SLD) but is used to describe difficulties that arise from deficits in one or more aspects of language including listening comprehension, oral language fluency, reading fluency, and writing fluency.

LANGUAGE-BASED TEACHING / INSTRUCTION is individualized or classroom instruction with the specific purpose of remediating or developing language and literacy skills.

LEXICON is the vocabulary of a language, a subject, or an individual speaker.

MORPHEMES are the smallest meaningful units of language. They are made up of phonemes (the individual speech sounds of language). A morpheme can be a complete word such as *walk* or *view*. It can also be a word part that creates the word's meaning such as *-ed, -ing, pre-*, etc.. For example, in the word *walked*, the word part *–ed* tells readers two things: 1) walk is a verb; and 2) the action happened in the past.

NEUROBIOLOGICAL DIFFERENCES are differences in the way an individual's brain processes stimulation including language.

NEUROPSYCHOLOGICAL EVALUATION refers to a series of diagnostic assessments and interviews with teachers, parents, and the student. Its purpose is to determine: what difficulties a student is experiencing; why; whether those difficulties are the result of a learning or other disability; and what educational interventions should be implemented to remediate the difficulties. A neuropsychological evaluation is similar to an educational evaluation, but assesses more cognitive and psychological areas of functioning, and is carried out by a neuropsychologist with input from as many individuals who work with the student as possible.

PHONEMES are the individual sound units that make up speech. The nonsense word *trate* is made up of four phonemes: /t/ + /r/ + /ā/ + /t/.

PHONOLOGICAL PROCESSING DISORDER describes an individual's difficulty identifying and manipulating the phonemes (separate speech sound units) within a word and/or learning how letters represent those sounds. The disorder is not related to hearing acuity, but to how the brain processes sound. It is commonly considered to be the underlying cause of most reading disorders.

PRAGMATICS refers to non-verbal forms of communication (e.g., facial expression, eye contact, volume, other body language). Sometimes called pragmatic language skills, or social communication skills, these non-verbal language skills are important to successful functioning in both the academic and social arenas. Students with weak pragmatic language skills are commonly misjudged as having poor manners, behavior problems, or emotional issues when, in fact, their pragmatic language skills are weak because of a language-based learning disability.

PROSODY refers to vocal intonations, rhythm, and stress that contribute to the meaning of words spoken or read aloud. Prosody gives a listener important information about what is being said, and it can alter the literal meaning of spoken words (e.g., sarcastic tone). Appropriate prosody while reading aloud can be a good indication of the reader's comprehension.

READING FLUENCY is the ability to read written language quickly, accurately, and with appropriate phrasing and expression (prosody) in order to grasp meaning.

SELF-ADVOCACY is the assertion or negotiation of one's interests, needs, and rights.

SELF-ASSESSMENT has two definitions. First, it is the evaluation of one's strengths and weaknesses in any given area. In addition, it refers to a form of classroom assessment in which students evaluate their own work according to a given set of criteria.

SELF-AWARENESS is the cognizance of one's own personality and character traits, unique strengths and weaknesses, feelings, and behaviors.

SELF-EFFICACY is the belief that one's actions are related to outcomes. A person who connects actions to positive outcomes will say, "I practice soccer every day. That helped me make the team," instead of, "I guess I got lucky." A person who connects actions to negative outcomes will say, "I forgot to bring my book home last night, so I couldn't read. That's why I failed the quiz today," not, "Those questions were too specific. The quiz was totally unfair." The idea of self-efficacy lies at the center of Albert Bandura's social-cognitive theory.

SEMANTICS are the meanings that correspond to words. Words may have denotative (literal) and connotative (associative) meanings. The word *ring* has multiple denotative meanings, both as a noun and a verb. It also has connotative meanings depending upon the context. Consider, for example, a ring given as a gift often connotes emotional commitment between the giver and the receiver. Certain types of rings connote different things such as marital engagement, membership in an organization, or pride in ethnic heritage for example.

SPEECH-LANGUAGE EVALUATION refers to a series of diagnostic assessments conducted by a speech-language pathologist (SLP) to determine the nature of an individual's difficulties with understanding and/or producing language.

SKILLS AND STRATEGIES are terms often used interchangeably, but they are actually different. A *strategy* is one specific approach to achieve a goal. For example, summarizing a chapter after reading is one strategy to aid in retention of the content. Other strategies may include highlighting, taking margin notes, making an outline, answering the questions at the end of the chapter, and creating index cards for vocabulary. A *skill* is the flexible and successful use of one or a combination of appropriate strategies in order to achieve a goal.

STUDY SKILLS is a term that refers to an array of organizational, learning, and memory strategies that empower individuals to manage materials, time, and language.

SYNTAX refers to the rules of grammar and sequence that create meaningful phrases and sentences.

VISUAL PROCESSING DISORDER causes difficulties with one or more of the following: visual discrimination; visual sequencing; visual motor processing; visual memory; visual closure; and spatial relationships. The disorder can underlie a variety of academic difficulties including reading and spelling.

Recommended Reading

The following list of books are recommended by the author as helpful resources for understanding and addressing diverse student needs in the classroom. Though this list is short, many outstanding resources are available in print and on the web.

Teaching

On Being a Teacher
Jonathan Kozol (Oneworld Publications)

The Influence of Teachers: Reflections on Teaching and Leadership
John Merrow (LM Books)

The Courage to Teach: Exploring the Inner Landscape of a Teacher's Life
Parker J. Palmer (Jossey-Bass)

Teaching for Wisdom, Intelligence, Creativity and Success
Robert Sternberg (Corwin Press)

Creating Innovators: The Making of Young People Who Will Change the World
Tony Wagner (Scribner)

Thinking, Learning, and Motivation Styles

Multiple Intelligences: New Horizons
Howard Gardner (Basic Books)

The Motivation Breakthrough: 6 Secrets to Turning On the Tuned-Out Child
Richard Lavoie (Simon and Schuster)

Drive: The Surprising Truth about What Motivates Us
Daniel Pink (Riverhead Books)

Thinking Styles
Robert Sternberg (Yale University Press)

Curriculum & Instructional Planning

Explicit Instruction: Effective and Efficient Teaching
Anita L. Archer and Charles A. Hughes (Guilford Press)

Teaching Content to All: Evidence Based Inclusive Practices in Middle and Secondary Schools
B. Keith Lenz, Donald D. Deshler, and Brenda R. Kissam (Allyn & Bacon)

Study Skills: Research Based Teaching Strategies & Study Skills Organizers
Patricia W. Newhall and Leigh Joseph (Landmark School, Inc.)

Teaching Independent Minds
Patricia W. Newhall (Landmark School, Inc.)

Teaching for Successful Intelligence: To Increase Student Learning and Achievement
Robert Sternberg and Elena Grigorenko (Corwin Press)

Integrating Differentiated Instruction & Understanding By Design: Connecting Content and Kids
Carol Ann Tomlinson and Jay McTighe (Association for Supervision and Curriculum Development)

Understanding By Design, Expanded 2nd Edition
Grant Wiggins and Jay McTighe (Prentice Hall)

Developing Oral and Written Language Skills

Multisensory Teaching of Basic Language Skills

Judith R. Birsh and Sally E. Shaywitz (Paul H. Brookes Publishing Company)

Scaffolded Writing Instruction: Teaching with a Gradual-Release Framework
Douglas Fisher and Nancy Frey (Scholastic Teaching Resources)

From Talking to Writing: Scaffolding Expository Expression
Terrill M. Jennings and Charles W. Haynes (Landmark School, Inc.)

Speech to Print: Language Essentials for Teachers
Louisa Cook Moats (Paul H. Brookes Publishing Company)

Thinking about Language: Helping Students Say What They Mean and Mean What They Say
Roberta Stacey (Landmark School, Inc.)

Developing Decoding & Reading Comprehension Skills

Informed Choices for Struggling Adolescent Readers: A Research-Based Guide to Instructional Programs and Practices
Donald Deshler, Annmarie Sullivan Palincsar, Gina Biancarosa, and Marnie Nair (International Reading Association)

Language and Reading Disabilties
Alan G. Kamhi and Hugh W. Catts (Allyn & Bacon)

Overcoming Dyslexia: A New and Complete Science-Based Program for Reading Problems at Any Level
Sally Shaywitz (Knopf)

Proust and the Squid: The Story and Science of the Reading Brain
Maryanne Wolf (Harper Perennial)

Executive Function & Attention Disorders

Executive Functions: What They Are, How They Work, and Why They Evolved
Russell A. Barkley (The Guilford Press)

Attention Deficit Disorder: The Unfocused Mind in Children and Adults
Thomas E. Brown (Yale University Press)

Executive Skills in Children and Adolescents:
A Practical Guide to Assessment and Intervention
Peg Dawson and Richard Guare (The Guilford Press)

Promoting Executive Function in the Classroom
Lynn Meltzer (The Guilford Press)

Mathematics

Why Is Math So Hard for Some Children? The Nature and Origins of Mathematical Learning Difficulties and Disabilities
Daniel B. Berch and Michele M.M. Mazzocco, eds. (Paul H. Brookes Publishing Company)

Teaching Mathematics to Middle School Students with Learning Difficulties
Marjorie Montague and Asha K. Jitendra (The Guilford Press)

Teaching Learners Who Struggle With Mathematics: Systematic Intervention and Remediation
Helene J. Sherman, Lloyd I. Richardson and George J. Yard (Prentice Hall)

References

Brooks, R. (2005, June). *The search for islands of competence: A metaphor of hope and strength*. Retrieved December 11, 2011, from http://www.dr-robertbrooks.com/writings/articles/0506.html

Brown, T. E. (n.d.). Welcome to DrThomasEBrown.com: A website that offers a new understanding of attention deficit disorder. Retrieved December 11, 2011, from http://www.drthomasebrown.com

Gardner, H. (1983). Frames of mind: The theory of multiple intelligences. New York: Basic Books.

Gardner, H. (2006). *Multiple intelligences: New horizons*. New York: Basic Books.

Goldberg, R. L. (2003). Predictors of Success in Individuals with Learning Disabilities: A Qualitative Analysis of a 20-Year Longitudinal Study. *Learning Disabilities Research & Practice (Blackwell Publishing Limited), 18*(4), 222.

McCloskey, G., Perkins, L. A., & Van Divner, B. (2008). *Assessment and intervention for executive function difficulties*. New York: Routledge.

Merton, R. K. (1968). The Matthew effect in science. *Science, 159*(3810): 56-63.

Palmer, P. J. (with Scribner, M.). (2007). *The courage to teach: Tenth anniversary edition*. San Franciso: Jossey-Bass.

PBS. (2002). *Misunderstood minds. Basics of mathematics*. Retrieved January 11, 2011, from http://www.pbs.org/wgbh/misunderstoodminds/math-basics.html

Project Zero. (2010). *Research projects*. Retrieved August 17, 2011, from Harvard University Web site: http://www.pz.harvard.edu/Research/Research.htm

Raskind, M. L. (2002). Teaching 'Life Success' to Students with LD: Lessons Learned From a 20-Year Study. *Intervention In School & Clinic, 37*(4), 201.

Shaywitz, S. (2003). Overcoming dyslexia: A new and complete science-based program for reading problems at any level. New York: Knopf.

Stacy, R. (2003). Thinking about language: Helping students say what they mean and mean what they say. Prides Crossing, MA: Landmark School, Inc.

Stanovich, K. E. (1986). Matthew effects in reading: Some consequences of individual differences in the acquisition of literacy. *Reading Research Quarterly 21*(4), 360-407.

Acknowledgments

This book is the result of Landmark Outreach's ongoing efforts to empower students through their teachers. It could not have been produced without the dedication and support of many people. Thanks to: Dan Ahearn for his commitment to putting useful information and strategies into teachers' hands, and his patience with the lengthy writing process; to Susan Tomases for organizing focus groups; to Anne Bellefeuille, Katie Hamon, Keryn Kwedor, Ann Larsen, and Dottie Seiter for their suggestions; to Liz Sweibel for her thorough editing; to my students (young people *and* adults) who continue to teach me how to be a better teacher; and to my children, John and Sarah, and their friends and friends' parents, who willingly share their stories about school and learning experiences.

About the Author

Patricia W. Newhall, M.A., M.S.Ed., is Associate Director of the Landmark School Outreach Program. A teacher of literature, writing, and study skills since 1987, she first joined the Landmark School faculty in 1993. In her publications and graduate courses, she shares research about learning disabilities and differences, and the teaching strategies essential to building the skills of struggling learners.

Newhall welcomes communication from fellow professionals and parents of struggling learners! Please feel free to contact her. Post comments and questions about this book, and about learning differences and teaching strategies on this book's homepage at www.landmarkoutreach.org/publications.